BIGFOOT
ENIGMA

SCOTT MARLOWE

Cover by Peter Loh

First published in the United States by Pangea Press

Pangea Press
514 Winter Terrace
Winter Haven, FL
33881

ISBN: 978-1492247241

Dedication

To the passionate and dedicated people who continue to pursue the identification and study of the creature known as "Bigfoot."

Contents

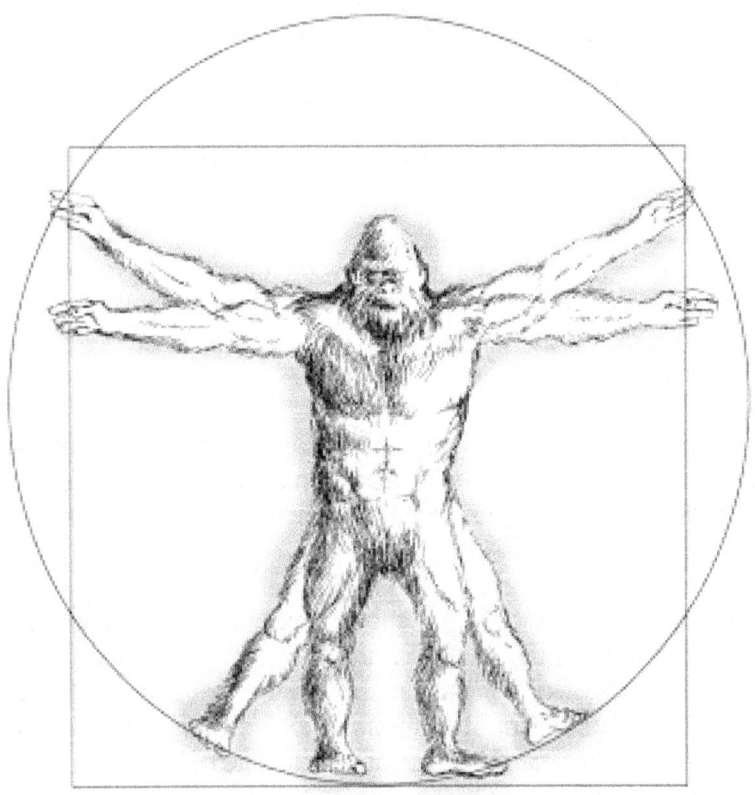

Introduction

The Dakota Native Americans have a saying: "We will be known forever by the tracks we leave." At first glance, this is certainly true of my Big Hairy Friend of the Forest -- Bigfoot.

Until recently, the main evidence in support of the existance of the animal were the many tracks found by woodsmen and women in numerous remote locations and, from time to time, nearby populated areas.

But, things have changed. Forensic science has given us new tools to uncover this mystery and the animal itself has left behind new physical evidence that even our latest laboratory wizardry can't explain away as anything else.

Certainly Bigfoot, in terms of circumstantial evidence, continues to mount support for its reality as a living being. Yet, mainstream science still regards the animal as a fiction unworthy of serious scientific study.

There is no need to convince those who believe in Bigfoot. Like the Anishinabe proverb, "What the people believe is true" -- to them at least. So, my purpose in writing this book is to, with hope, plant some doubt in those who are convinced that "we know everything" and that no animal the size of Bigfoot could go undetected in today's electronic world with it advanced surveillance technologies.

One mainstream scientist that I can't help but respect, Jane Goodall, has the proper attitude towards this subject and isn't afraid to say so publically, "there are people looking. There are very ardent groups in Russia, and they have published a whole lot of stuff about what they've seen. Of course, the big criticism of all this is, 'Where is the body?' You know, why isn't there a body? I can't answer that, and maybe they don't exist, but I want them to."

Wanting isn't enough. Dr. Goodall knows that. But, she has a scientific mind that is open to possibilities. This is as it should be in science.

So, perhaps the Arapaho are right, "If we wonder often, the gift of knowledge will come." A little doubt might just be enough to make people wonder . . .

What is Bigfoot?

There are a number of hypotheses that attempt to explain the mysterious creature commonly known as "Bigfoot." Indeed, the continuing debate as regards this animal is often at the forefront of hominology around the world. But, the domestic debates frequently do not take into account that beasts of a similar description exist in the myth, legend and folklore of indigenous peoples around the world — if not in reality.

There are basically six schools of thought on what "Bigfoot" actually is.

The classic, and somewhat romantic theory, is that the creature is an undiscovered animal not currently known (i.e. not an. scientifically described) within mainstream science.

Then there are those that believe the animal is a relic hominin (i.e. a forerunner of modern man). A slight variation of this thought considers the creature to be an obscure human "tribe" of hirsute hermits.

Still others dismiss the creature as simply fantasy and folklore while yet another group believes that "Sightings" of this "creature: are just a case of mistaken identity where the animal is known to science, but the species reported is simply out of its normal element and the people seeing it attribute their "sighting" to the mythical "Bigfoot."

Of course the final version arises from people who try to hoax or "punk" others with a contrived fraud -- usually with a profit motive.

Indeed, most of these ideas have been revealed in the past as possibilities, but all are (perhaps mistakenly) held to the standard of the "Undiscovered Animal" hypothesis.

Regardless of the hypothesis, most all of the concepts as to the creature's actuality hold that the animal is some sort of primate — specifically a great ape of some type.

There are ursid-, simioid-, pongid-, and hominin-like, Bigfoot creatures reported on every temperate continent. These body types are often encountered where these creatures are "seen" and are typically associated with the body mass and general appearance of the animal's head. These traits are immediately apparent to an eyewitness — even at a distance.

TYPICAL BIGFOOT BODY TYPES

URSID-LIKE   SIMIAN-LIKE   PONGID-LIKE   HOMININ-LIKE

Fig. 1 - *Bigfoot creatures are generally reported as appeaing similar to a bipedal bear, chimpanzee, gorilla or primative human.*

These descriptive differences suggest that there may be more than one species of "Bigfoot" being seen by eyewitnesses. But these descriptions, by themselves, do not constitute sufficient evidence to conclude that this is true. However, other evidence that I will present here does suggest that multiple species of undiscovered primates do exist.

For the purposes of this work, I will concentrate on the anthropoid vertebrates that belong to this array of cryptid bipeds and collectively refer to them as "Bigfoot" or "BHPs" (Bipedal Hairy Primates). However, the reader should take note that this terminology is merely a convenience and not intended to state that these creatures are of the same species.

An in-depth examination of the material associated with Bigfoot not only suggests that there are several species of Bigfoot, but that some of these animals may not even belong of the same genus.

Enigmatic anthropoid creatures are known by a myriad of colloquial names around the world.

Thus, it seems prudent to begin this report with a catalogue of the known terms used to specify these cryptid animals throughout the world.

Name	Region/Country	Continent	Size
Abnauayu	Caucasus	Asia	Moderate
Agogwe	Tanzania	Africa	Dwarf
Aigypan	Venezuela	South America	Moderate
Almas	Caucasus	Asia	Moderate
Almasty	Caucasus	Asia	Moderate
Alux	Yucatan	North America	Dwarf
Apamandi	Zaire	Africa	Dwarf
Arulataq	Alaska	North America	Moderate
Barmanou	Pakistan/Afghanistan	Asia	Moderate
Batutut	Borneo	Asia	Dwarf
Big Greg Man	Scotland	Europe	Moderate
Bigfoot	Northwestern USA	North America	Moderate
Bili Ape	Congo	Africa	Moderate
Brenin Llwyd	Scotland	Europe	Moderate
Chemosit	Kenya	Africa	Moderate
Chimanimani	South Africa	Africa	Dwarf
Chuchunaa	Siberia	Asia	Moderate
Curinquean	South America	South America	Giant
Didi	Guyana	South America	Dwarf
Duende	Peru	South America	Dwarf
Dzu-Teh	Himalayas	Asia	Giant
Fating'ho	Senegal	Africa	Dwarf
Ferla Mohr	Scotland	Europe	Moderate
Gin-Sung	China	Asia	Giant
Grendel	Denmark	Europe	Moderate
Guayazi	South America	South America	Dwarf
Gul-Biavan	Russia/Mongolia	Asia	Moderate
Higabon	Japan	Asia	Dwarf
Honey Island Swamp Monster	Louisiana	North America	Moderate
Jungli Admi	India	Asia	Dwarf
Kapre	Philippines	Asia	Dwarf
Kaptar	Russia/Mongolia	Asia	Moderate
Khi-Trau	Laos/Vietnam	Asia	Moderate
Kikomba	Zaire	Africa	Moderate
Koolookamba	Gabon	Africa	Dwarf
Ksy-Giik	Kazakhstan/Kirghizistan	Asia	Moderate
Kung-Lu	China	Asia	Giant
Macro	New Zealand	Oceania	Dwarf
Maero	New Zealand	Oceania	Dwarf
Mapinguary	Brazil	South America	Moderate
Mau	East Africa	Africa	Dwarf
Mawas	Malaysia	Asia	Moderate

Name	Region/Country	Continent	Size
Meh-teh	Himalayas	Asia	Moderate
Menehune	Hawaii	Oceania	Dwarf
Metoh-Kangmi	Nepal	Asia	Moderate
Momo	Missouri	North America	Moderate
Mono Grande	Guyana	South America	Dwarf
Moehau	New Zealand	Oceania	Moderate
Mono Rei	Venezuela	South America	Moderate
Muhalu	West Africa	Africa	Moderate
Nasnas	Iran	Asia	Moderate
Nguoi Rung	Vietnam	Asia	Moderate
Nittaewo	Sri Lanka	Asia	Dwarf
Orang Dalam	Sumatra	Asia	Moderate
Orang Gadang	Sumatra	Asia	Giant
Orang Gugu	Philippines	Asia	Moderate
Orang Kubu	Sumatra	Asia	Moderate
Orang Sanat	Sumatra	Asia	Moderate
Orang Pendek	Sumatra	Asia	Dwarf
Rakshasa	Nepal	Asia	Moderate
Sehité	Ivory Coast	Africa	Dwarf
Shiru	Colombia	South America	Dwarf
Sisemite	Guatemala/Belize	North America	Moderate
Skunk Ape	Florida	North America	Moderate
Swamp Ape	Southeastern USA	North America	Moderate
Susquatch	Canada	North America	Moderate
Tano Giant	West Africa	Africa	Moderate
Tarma	Peru	South America	Dwarf
Teh-lma	Himalayas	Asia	Dwarf
Tok	China	Asia	Giant
Tokoloshe	Southern Rhodesia	Africa	Dwarf
Tree Eater	Finland/Croatia	Europe	Moderate
Ucu	Chile	South America	Moderate
Ucumar	Chile	South America	Moderate
Ufiti	Malawi	Africa	Dwarf
Ukumarzupai	Argentina/Chile	South America	Moderate
Vasitri	Venezuela	South America	Moderate
Vedi	Croatia	Europe	Dwarf
Véle	Fiji Islands	Asia	Dwarf
Wa'ab	Sudan	Africa	Moderate
Waray-Waray	Eastern Samar	Asia	Moderate
Wookie	Louisiana	North America	Moderate
Windigo	Quebec	North America	Moderate
Wudewasa	Finland	Europe	Moderate
Xipe	Nicaragua	South America	Dwarf

Name	Region/Country	Continent	Size
Yeh-Ren	China	Asia	Moderate
Yahoo	New Zealand	Oceania	Moderate
Yeti	Nepal	Asia	Moderate
Yowie	Australia	Oceania	Moderate

*Note that this catalog of names is not complete and that I am adding new designations to this list as I discover them. Moreover, some of the creatures denoted by the term provided may be equivocal as to their status as applies to the generality attribution of this work.

BIGFOOT HEIGHT COMPARISONS

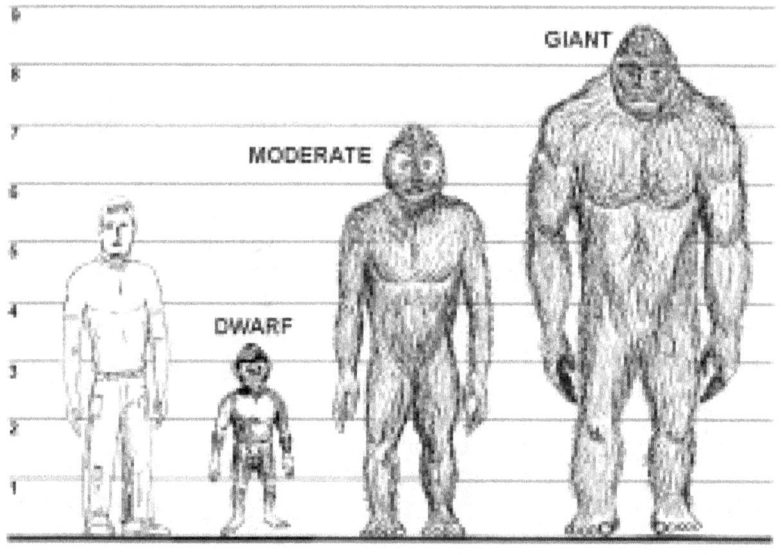

Fig. 2 - *In this chart of height comparison of BHPs, we can see the large variation of reported heights attributed to these animals by eyewitnesses from around the world.*

Another of the animal's obvious bodily characteristics is the creatures physical stature. There are three height categories for "Bigfoot" or Bipedal Hairy Primates (BHPs) known around the world.

In the table above, man-sized Bigfoot (5 to 8 feet tall) are listed as "Moderate". "Dwarf" or pygmy (not to be confused with the Pygmy

Bushmen of Africa) Bigfoot are approximately 3 to 4 feet in height, and "Giant" Bigfoot, who stand in at 8 feet tall or more.

n addition to the height variations, each BHP creature manifests certain obvious variations in the color of body hair ranging from black or dark brown, to reddish brown, tan or blonde, and grey or silver white.

A stucy, compiled by Mike Phillips, from several Bigfoot sighting databases reports that the coloration attributed to the anima; falls into one of the above categories with some variations by geographical area on the North American continent. Unfortunately, I am not aware of similar studies pertaining to the creature elsewhere in the world. But, I suspect that the findings and color distrubution would be similar.

East of the Mississippi

The Southeast, (AL, FL, GA, KY, MS, NC, SC, & TN)

Black/brown	88	62%
Red/brown	23	16%
Tan/blonde	6	4%
Grey/White	25	18%

The Middle Atlantic (VA, WV, MD, & DE)

Black/brown	19	67%
Red/brown	1	4%
Tan/blonde	3	11%
Grey/white	5	18%

The Northeast. (New England States, PA, NY, & NJ)

Black/brown	52	69%
Red/brown	5	7%
Tan/blonde	7	09%
Grey/white	11	15%

Tbe Rust Belt"(OH, IL, IN, WI, & MI)

Black/brown	100	68%
Red/brown	14	10%
Tan/blonde	7	5%
Grey/white	26	17%

West of the Mississippi

The Lower Midwest (AR, LA, TX, & OK)

Black/brown	100	55%
Red/brown	43	24%
Tan/blonde	9	5%
Grey/white	30	16%

The Upper Midwest (KS, MO, NE, Iowa, ND, SD, MN, & WI)

Black/brown	36	64%
Red/brown	10	18%
Tan/blonde	6	11%
Grey/white	5	7%

The Mountain West (AZ, CO, ID MT, NM, UT,

Black/brown	70	74%
Red/brown	6	6%
Tan/blonde	9	9%
Grey/white*	10	11%

*Grey/white not reported in MT, ID, or WY

The West Coast (CA, O, WA, and BC)

Black/brown	195	77%
Red/brown	34	13%
Tan/blonde	12	5%
Grey/white	14	5%

Canada

Provinces East of British Columbia

Black/brown	29	77%
Red/brown	2	5%
Tan/blonde	2	5%
Grey/white	5	13%

To critique Mr. Phillip's results, some variation in these figures is to be expected because not all color descriptions are exact. Some witnesses describe a grey/brown or a dark grey creature. Others describe a Bigfoot that is partly red/brown or darker brown. In these cases choices were made about how to record the sighting data. The researcher expects that the black/brown category is under represented.

Many witnesses state they first thought they saw a bear but never mention coloration in their account. In these cases the researcher assumed that it was unlikely that the creature reported was anything but black or brown, but, didn't count these in the totals here.

These are updated figures through 2004, including new sightings which have been posted since the researcher began mining the database for these figures.

BIGFOOT HAIR COLORATION

North America

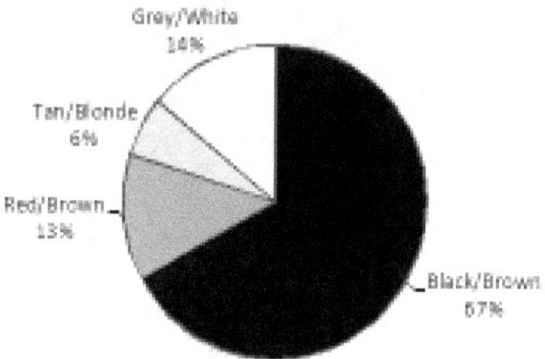

Fig. 3 - Combining the count data from Mr. Phillip's study results in the pie chart of hair color distribution above for the North American continent (excluding Mexico)

So, for North America the variation of hair coloration for Bigfoot creatures in total is represented by the pie chart appearing above. Of interest here is that these colorations are not unusual for primates. Indeed, they fall well within human norms and are manifest in other great apes, most notably the gorilla family and chimpanzees.

Other physical traits are often not as apparent and include variations in foot anatomy, facial physiognomy, limb length, posture, and diet. Of course, gender can be apparent although in some sightings, it is not immediately so.

Additionally, there are some notable differences in the behavioral attributes among these creatures beyond the obvious commonality of being rare and reclusive beasts.

I will elaborate further on physiological and behavioral characteristics as well as other factors that appear to impact classification criteria separately later in this work.

For now, I would like to focus on typical accounts of human encounters with these animals and begin by formulating some initial impressions about them from these accounts.

Brief Glimpses

The distinction of being the first white man to encounter physical Bigfoot evidence in the Americas belongs to David Thompson.

Thompson reported some unusual animal footprints measuring some fourteen inches in length and eight inches wide. The tracks left four discernible toe impressions and were found in the snow during the winter of 1811. Mr. Thompson was a trader who claimed to have discovered tracks made by a Sasquatch (the term "Bigfoot" wasn't coined until 1958) near what now is the town of Jasper in Alberta, Canada. (The track would have resembled the example footprint that appears on the right).

While Thompson didn't report that he actually saw the animal that made the tracks, this incident is nevertheless accepted as the first recorded North American discovery of clear physical evidence left behind by one of these elusive creatures.

A more current "sighting" occurred along a stretch of County Road 92 near Marco Island, Florida at around 9:00PM in early January of 2005. Jerry Churba, a resident of Naples, Florida, reported the incident in a Marco Island Sun Times issue dated January 13, 2005.

Churba said, "I tend to be skeptical of unusual animal sightings. However when a close friend recently had an encounter at night with a 'tall, thin, nude man with long hair' that was loping across Highway 92, my skepticism was shattered." (See photograph below for a "reenactment" of the reported scene).

Churba's friend was returning home when she was about three miles southeast of the Goodland Bridge that connects the mainland with Marco Island. The roadway in that part of the highway is actually a narrow two-lane causeway with water on either side of the road. Beyond the water is extensive mangrove swamp and islands within a short swim from the grassy median on either side of the pavement.

The "nude man" bounded from the left-hand side of the road to right, across the highway in front of the car the woman was driving. However, when Churba's friend neared the area where she had seen the "person", there was no one in sight. She had no doubt that the momentum of forward movement propelled the "man" into the water.

There were no other cars on the highway at the time and no cars parked along the shoulder of the road (the area is a popular fishing spot with local sportsmen). There are no human habitations along that stretch of highway and the surrounding mangrove swamp is uninhabited, dark and foreboding.

This account provides a location, date, time of day and vague description of the animal. The gender of the beast was determined by observable genitalia.

Having investigated this sighting personally, I am somewhat dubious as to the reliability of this particular report. First, there is a proximity issue in that this location is close to the "stomping grounds" of a known "Skunk Ape" hoaxter. In a similar incident that took place in 2003, two female Europeans on vacation in the nearby Big Cypress Swamp were surprised by "a huge male Skunk Ape" with an erection. The coincidence of the "observable genitalia" is all too obvious.

Additionally the release of a video product, *The Ochopee Skunk Ape,* which debuted in April of 2005 at the Bombay Club on Marco Island, Florida raises the probability of a publicity stunt to promote sales of the DVD.

Nevertheless, other reports of Bigfoot activity bear a striking resemblance to the Marco Island story line.

In another encounter that occurred at the North end of the State, Bill Arnold was driving down Highway 65 in the Florida Panhandle.

At 6:00 PM on May 17, 2004, Arnold was headed toward Saint George Island, Florida along the roadway and saw what appeared to be a Bigfoot (AKA "Swamp Ape") creature in a location known as Tate's Hell Swamp (See reenactment photo on the right).

The creature crossed the road about 100 yards ahead of him and Mr. Arnold was unable to discern the gender of the animal from that distance. However, Mr. Arnold did note that the animal paid little attention to his oncoming truck while crossing the roadway.

In Central Florida, Pat Edwards encountered a Swamp Ape while driving

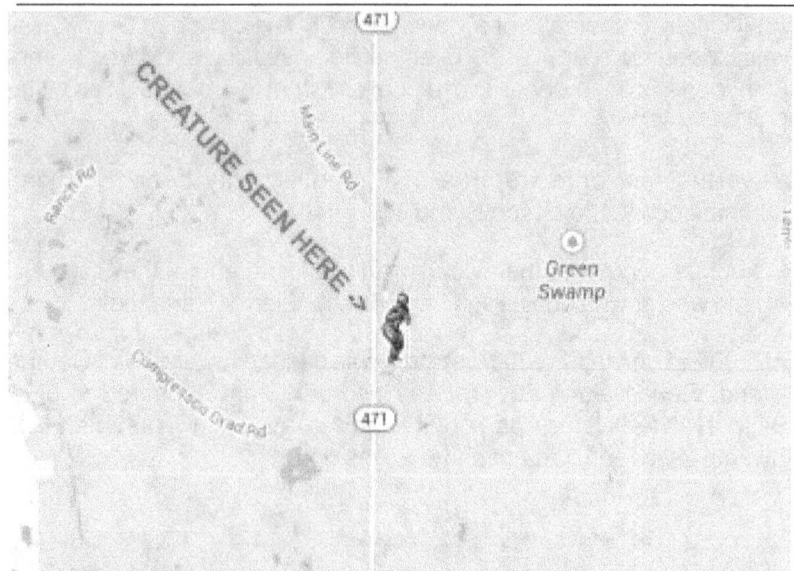

along County Road 471 from US Route 98 near Lakeland to Webster, Florida and the nearby National Cemetery in the October of 2002. The area of her encounter was in the Green Swamp Wildlife Management District south of the Richloam Tract.

Like the Marco Island account, the animal quickly crossed the road, dove into an adjacent canal and disappeared.

In more than one instance a Florida Bigfoot was struck by a car or truck, but apparently survived — running off and disappearing into the night.

Steven Humphreys reported one such encounter with a Swamp Ape. The creature was running across road on a Martin County, Florida highway in 1975 when a very surprised Humphreys struck it. There was considerable damage to Humphreys' car, which was documented photographically by his insurance company, but he could find no sign of the hairy victim of the accident when he had stopped to render aid immediately after the impact.

There are other encounters documented in Florida going back to 1942 in my collection of sighting reports. Other research organizations that track sightings of BHP creatures throughout the world have files that contain hundreds of similar stories involving momentary encounters with Bigfoot- like animals similar to the ones I've mentioned above. In fact, most encounters with a BHP animal are sudden and unexpected glimpses of the beast that offer little detailed information about its

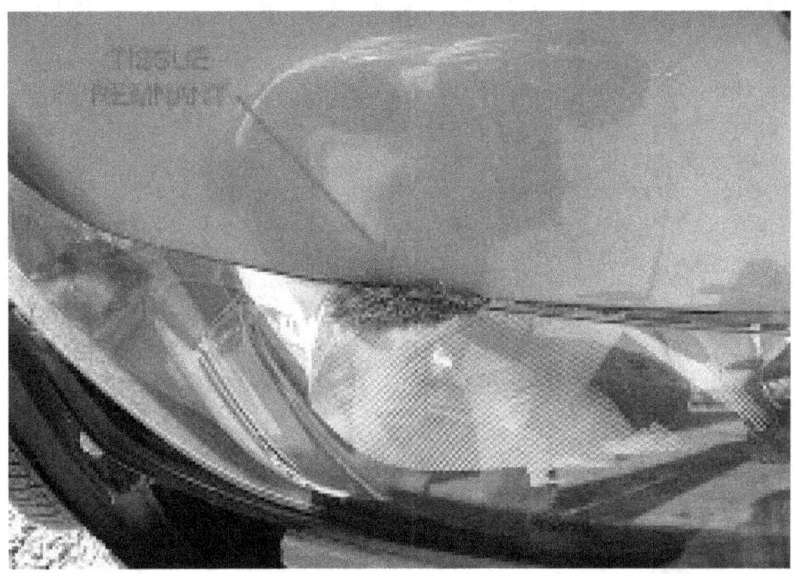

Note the hair and tissue sample imbedded between the headlight and canopy of this car after a collision with a deer. Similar material should result from accidents involving a reported Bigfoot.

appearance or behaviors. Many times, the experience is so sudden or frightful that the observer's description of the animal is likely to be distorted or incomplete.

By and large these accounts are hearsay and wouldn't hold up in a court of law due to a lack of physical evidence and they have no scientific value at all in proving the existence of these animals — as should be the case with strictly anecdotal accounts of BHP sightings. In these instances, the investigator is required to treat the account as not factual. In other cases, a sighting is clearly credible, but of little use in filling in the blanks that permeate the legends about the animal.

More to the point, when accidents yield an opportunity for tissue or blood sampling it would seem logical to require that law enforcement optain samples from the damaged automobile or truck. In this day and age of DNA testing, physical evidence of this type would offer conclusive proof of the struck animal's identity. Nevertheless, from such accounts, one can begin to assemble a profile of the animal's physiology and behavior — much like a criminologist develops a criminal profile to solve a crime case.

Despite the anecdotal sources, verbal information obtained from the reports previously mentioned allow us to infer that the Florida Swamp Ape is able to swim and has no fear of the denizens that also live in the swampy environment prevalent in this geography. Another obvious logical conclusion is that, it is unlikely that these encounters would involve the same animal, given the distance from one sighting location to another, so it follows that more than one of them exists in a large geographical area. It also follows that, since both genders are regularly sighted, and on occasion, an adult is seen with a child, that it is a safe bet that these animals breed and bear offspring.

Other inferences are not so evident. For example, when you take credible reports as a group, and look at them over time, these accounts can also provide a glimpse into the possible migration patterns of these animals and suggest a range within which they wander — a hypothesis that can be tested.

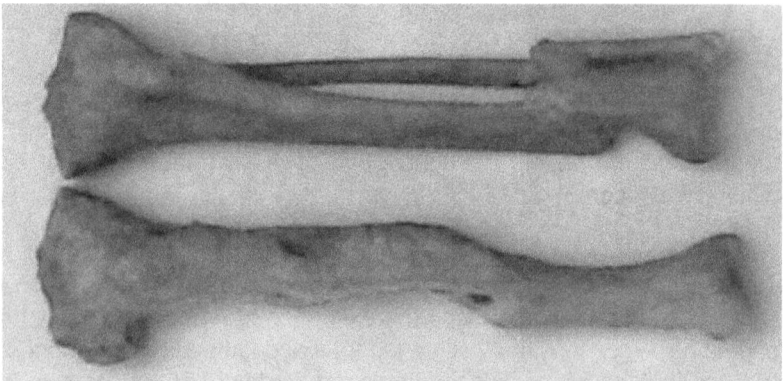

Fig. 4 - *Pathologically deformed lower leg bones from a Homo sapiens This individual had both legs broken very badly in an accident. However, he survived long enough for the bones to re-heal, although they became badly offset. The bones of the right leg show that he also developed a massive infection that produced extreme deformities in the re-healed bone.*

Since there are multiple stories of the animal being struck by vehicles ranging from sports cars to large trucks, we can also infer that the animal has a high pain tolerance and resilience. This is a trait that anthropologists assign to at least one human ancestor, Homo neandertalensis as several skeletons of this hominin have been found where the living creature sustained considerable injury and survived.

Neanderthal fossil remains demonstrate that the wounds healed subsequent to the injury of the living Neanderthal, which had a denser bone structure than its Homo sapiens counterpart.

Indeed, some modern humans exhibit this pain resilience trait. Rodeo riders often have sustained injuries similar to those found in some Neanderthal remains and have simply gotten back on their feet to continue their competition.

More to the point, even in accidents involving animals where a carcass is not available at the scene, law enforcement or insurance companies should collect blood and tissue samples from the damaged automobile or truck for laboratory testing. In this day and age of DNA technology, physical evidence of this type would likely lead to conclusive proof of BHP involvement where such contact is reported.

Credible Encounters

The story of William Roe's encounter with what appears to have been a Sasquatch or Bigfoot contains some of the first detailed observations about the animal. In a sworn statement, given on August 26, 1957, Roe, whose various occupations included hunting, trapping, and road labor, was working in British Columbia at the time of his reported encounter. Roe told of the event that occurred in the year 1955. He had hiked alone five miles up Mica Mountain, near Valemount, Canada to explore a deserted mine.

Upon stepping out into a clearing, Roe observed an animal that he initially thought was a grizzly bear. But, when the animal stood erect, he immediately perceived that the animal was "obviously not a bear." The animal, a female (he had noticed its mammary glands), was about six feet in height and approximately three feet wide. He estimated that it weighed around 300 pounds. The animal's arms hung down almost

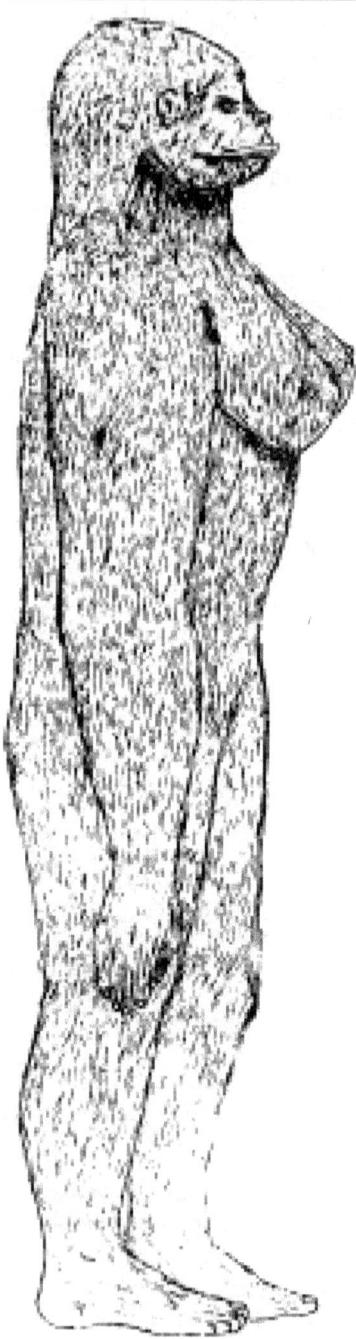

to her knees. She was bipedal and walked putting the heel of the foot down first as does a human.

Roe concealed himself in some underbrush and quietly watched the animal from a distance of about seven yards. He reported that she used her white, even teeth to consume leaves from a nearby bush. The animal's skull appeared "higher at the back than at the front" and the nose was flat. "Only the area around her mouth was bare - the rest of her body was covered in hair, none of which was longer than an inch." The animal's ears looked very human and its eyes were small and dark, similar in appearance to those of a bear.

Unfortunately, the animal evidently became aware of Roe's scent as the wind shifted. At which point, it walked back the way it had apparently come, looking over back as it made its way back into the forest.

As it withdrew into the woods, Roe could hear it make a vocalization that he said was "a kind of a whinny".

Fig. 5 - *This drawing was made by William Roe's daughter three years after his encounter in 1955 at his direction. Some Bigfoot researchers think that Roe's report became an inspiration for Roger Patterson and thus believe that his famous Bluff Creek encounter with "Patty" was faked.*

Roe's experience as a hunter helped him remain levelheaded. To ascertain whether the animal was herbivorous or carnivorous, he looked for scat (feces) in the area around the sighting location. He found samples and inspected them but could not detect hair or insect shells. So, he concluded that the animal survived on vegetation alone.

Roe didn't claim that the animal he observed was a "Bigfoot" (that term didn't come into use until 1958), or a "Sasquatch" (the Native American Indian term meaning "hairy giant" that had been used for centuries to describe the kind of beast Roe observed). But his account is one of the earliest credible, modern day sightings of this animal on the North American continent.

We are fortunate that Mr. Roe's keen observation skills and close proximity to the animal allowed him to provide some intimate details about the elusive Bigfoot creature.

Shortly after Hurricane Charley rampaged through her Lakeland, Florida neighborhood on August 13, 2004, Jennifer Ward, a thirty year old mother of two, was driving north, back to her home up Moore Road, a normally well-traveled rural byway located in northern Polk County. The storm had left the area flooded, but the road was still passable at the time Ms. Ward was driving it in her SUV.

As she was driving along, she saw something crouching down in the flooded drainage gully on the left-hand side of the road, near the intersection of Tom Costine Road, where she would make a left turn to get to the street where she resides.

As she neared the animal, it stood up on two legs when it saw her vehicle approach. The animal assumed a timid posture as it watched Jennifer drive by — cutting off it's only means of escape into the wooded area across the street from which it had apparently come.

Jennifer describes the animal as a creature with a human form that was covered in dark hair or fur. She estimates the height of the animal at 8 feet tall and suggests that the creature was foraging in the ditch when she came upon it.

"It looked like it was doing something; it was focused on something," Ward says. "When it saw me, it took on my facial expressions and seemed as dumbfounded as I was. It just watched me as I drove by."

Jennifer, who with her husband, is an avid outdoors person and is very familiar with the animals of the Green Swamp where she lives, insists that the creature was "definitely not a bear."

Ward didn't stop to observe for a longer period of time because her two daughters were sleeping in the back seat of her Toyota 4-Runner and she feared that the animal might attack if given the chance.

However, Jennifer quickly drove to her home and returned to the site with her camera — hoping that the animal would stick around and

Fig. 6 - *Drawn from Ms. Ward's memory, this forensic rendering by artist Matt Ellis records the eyewitness description of the animal she saw.*

search for hair or footprints at the scene.

She did find animal scat, which she photographed, but missed a lock of hair that I later found entangled in the barbed wire fence across the street. (This was after Hurricane Frances passed through the area about three-weeks later - after I was asked to investigate the sighting by her husband Richard). I determined that the hair was most likely human — noticing that, under a microscope that the hair had been cut with a sharp instrument and that it didn't have follicles attached to the roots making further testing of the sample for species identification unwarranted.

Jennifer did find unusual tracks on her grandfather's ranch, adjacent to the area of her sighting, the next day and photographed these footprints — taking care to date and time stamp the digital photos. I later determined that these tracks were consistent with those taken in the Ocala National Forest after sighting events that have occurred since 1987.

The dung appeared to be that of a canine and since Jennifer had not collected the material for analysis, thus no further study of the contents or DNA extraction could be performed.

However, Jennifer's two or three minute encounter with the Swamp Ape at close range did offer one startling observation — Jennifer reported that the animal had whitish "rings" around its eyes. At first, this description was not well-received by the Bigfoot community — until I pointed out that there is a precedent for this trait within the ranks of New World monkey species. This is also somewhat similar to the appearance of the famous de Loys ape photograph which we will further discuss at a later place in this work..

Fig 7 - *Squirrel monkeys live in Central and South America and possess the "white ring" trait described by Jennifer Ward in her Swamp Ape. Old World primates like the Macaque of Asia also exhibit this physical trait.*

*DeLoys' famed
ape photo*

Then there is the account of Albert Ostman who, while on a camping trip in the vicinity of Vancouver Island in western Canada in 1924: finding that some animal had rumaged through his gear and food stores over two consecutive evenings.

Late one night Mr. Ostman awoke to discover that he was being roughly carried off while still inside his sleeping bag. Mr. Ostman had little chance of escape and was dragged along the forest floor for about 25 miles while he nearly suffocated because the opening of his sleeping bag was held shut by his kidnapper until he was thossed to the ground. When Mr. Ostman was finally able to exit the sleeping roll, he found himself among a Sasquatch family unit with an adult male and female and their two offspring. He reported that the adult male who abducted him was over eight feet in height and very muscular and that the younger animals were shorter, but still about seven feet in height.

Apparently able to communicate with each other, the group did not harm or threaten him, but they prevented him from leaving their company. They lived in the open inside a small mastif enclosed by cliffs on three sides. The elder male guarded the entrance to enclosure. Although he wasn't sure, Mr. Ostman speculated that he was intended to be "breading stock" for the younger female.

Mr. Ostman's ordeal lasted six days and was only able to escape when he offered tobacco snuff to the large male who dumped the contents of the container into his mouth incapacitating the animal long enough to permit Ostman the opportunity to run away. Mr. Ostman didn't tell anyone about his encounter until 1957 when he felt that the public might be ready to believe him.

On September 26, 1997 a story broke in China involving a man who had a cranium that appeared to be somewhat smaller than usual and sported a vestigial tail. He was about 7 feet tall and walked with an unusually wide gait. His body shape was distinctive and his extremities were a bit longer than normal. The man lacked long body hair and did not or could not speak. The subject was discovered in the Shennongjjia region of China which known for its remote forests and as a location where many rare animals can be found.

At the time of his video debut, the man was thought to be about 33 years old. What was curious about this incident was that the mother of the man had been a widow for a long time and claimed that, after the passing of her husband, she was abducted by a Yeren, a Chinese Bigfoot or "Wildman", who had been the "sire" the "boy." The mother of the man didn't come forward about her abduction sooner because of the shame of what had happened to her.

Now, the woman had previously born a son by her human husband. That son was then an officer in the Red Army and he had prevailed upon his mother to tell her story to the Wildlife Research Organization of China who had 0righinally broken the story.

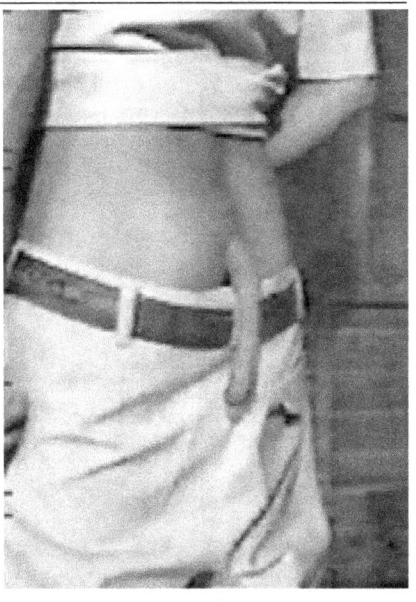

Fig. 8 - *Atavistic structures in particular individuals arise from a defect in the animal's genetic development. A gene simply doesn't turn on (or off) at the proper time during fetal development.*

However vestigial organs, like the appendix, are genetic holdovers from a species' ancestors. These occur in all members of a species and the organ has lost its original

Living Among Us

It should be noted at this point in this report that, as of this writing, living specimens of the Almas (or Almasty), Yeti, Mono Rei and the N'goloko (now known to be the "Bili Ape") constitute well-documented instances where "Bigfoot" animals have had direct interaction with people.

In the case of the Almas, a zoologist by the name of Alexander Mashkovtsev, heard and studied the story of Zana, an Almas or Yeti captured in the Western Caucasus region of what is now the independent states of Armenia, Azerbaijan, and The Republic of Georgia.

Fig. 9 - *Zana was apparently captured in the Och'amch'ire district of the Abkhazia region of today's Republic of Georgia in a mountainous area by a group of hunters.*

Zana lived and past on sometime during the latter half of the nineteenth century —within the life span of a number of villagers with whom she neighbored. These eyewitnesses were still alive at the time of Mashkovtsev's research and were interviewed by him.

Subsequent to Mr. Mashkovtsev's investigation, Boris Porshnev published The Struggle for Troglodytes in which he details Zana's story.

The manner in which Zana was captured is equivocal. Some accounts have her being inadvertently found in the wilds, while other reports state that she had been captured by design. But details of her seizure are perfunctory to the fact that she eventually came into the possession of Edgi Genaba, a nobleman of this region.

At first, Zana was kept in an enclosure and had limited human contact. Her food was simply thrown to her. Her keepers reported that she dug holes to sleep in. However, after about three years, she grew accustomed to humans and was allowed out of her pen and eventually permitted to roam about the rural district.

Zana's skin color was black, or a dark gray. Her entire body was covered with reddish-black hair. The hair on her head was unkempt and thick and hung like a horse's mane down her back.

Zana could not, or would not, speak but made unintelligible sounds and grumbles. She did cry out when she was irritated or frustrated. Zana would acknowledge when called by her name and could follow simple commands given by her master. After she became accustomed to humans, she would become timid and obviously frightened when her master shouted at her.

Zana was unusually tall, imposing and broad. She possessed huge breasts and buttocks, muscular arms and legs. Her fingers were longer and thicker than the digits of a "normal" human and she could flare out her toes and splay the big toe farther than is usual.

Despite aging, Zana's hair did not go gray. She did not loose teeth, and remained strong and fit throughout her life. Her athletic stamina was enormous. She could outrun a horse and easily swim across a local River — even when it would occasionally rise in a violent high tide. She climbed trees to harvest fruit, and would gorge herself on grapes. She had a colossal appetite and ate whatever food she was given, which typically included porridge and meat, without benefit of utensils.

Zana preferred the cold and often would lie down in a cool pool side by side with wild ox and bison. She was known to roam the surrounding hills at nighttime. Zana sometime would wield wooden clubs when fell upon by dogs and in other situations when she felt in peril. When angry Zana presented a grotesque spectacle and would bite if she got the opportunity.

She also had a peculiar obsession to trifle with stones, striking one against the other to split them into pieces – apparently attempting to imitate the knapping skill necessary to flake a lithic tool from the rock material (see illustration below left).

She preferred to wander around naked — even in winter – and would tear clothing that she was given into shreds. She did, however, demonstrate a tolerance for a loincloth.

Despite her primitive customs, Zana was successfully trained to perform some elementary domestic tasks like grinding grain into flour, fetching firewood and carrying water from a well. She also hauled heavy sacks of flour to and from the local mill with ease.

Striking stones together (knaoping) is a skill common to neolighic man for the purpose of making crude stone tools

The accounts of Zana agree that she had an attachment to wine. This fondness for drink led to a number of pregnancies by a variety of men from her village. Zana had at least six children exhibiting typical Homo sapiens characteristics at birth. She bore her offspring without the assistance of doctors or midwives.

Zana engaged an interesting behavior of immersing her newborn in a cold water spring. This practice is evidently similar to that of Scandinavian cultures which is said to produce hardy offspring and akin to the legend surrounding the birth of the Greek hero Achilles of legend.

Zana's first two offspring died because of this immersion, but the last four children survived when they were rescued from this dunking ritual by several village women who took charge of the children.

Of these four, there were two boys and two girls. The children grew up to be like the villagers, with some slight physiological differences. Each of these children went on to become parents and their descendants now live throughout the region. Zana's children were named: Dzhanda, a male, born in 1878, Kodzhanar, a female, born in 1880, Gamasa Sabekia, a female, born in 1882, and Khwit Sabekia, a male, born around 1884. (The latter two of these children were given a surname by the wife of Zana's owner who raised them).

After her death, Zana was buried near her village at T'khina in the central part of the Och'amch'ire District of Abkhazia sometime during in the 1880s or 1890s. Thus, her existence (as reported by the eyewitnesses) and zoological status could presumably be confirmed by locating her gravesite and exhuming her corpse.[1]

The significance of Zana's story is genetic – she would have to have been a closely related member of the hominin family tree if not an anomaly belonging to our own species. Some cryptozoologists and Russian anthropologists speculate that she was a Neanderthal. It would be interesting to have Zana's descendants examined to ascertain their genetic attributes and lineage to confirm Mashkovtsev's and Porshney's accounts through contemporary DNA testing.[1]

Zana's children, Gamasa and Khwit, were both powerfully built, and had the dark skin coloration of their mother. However, they inherited very little else, physiologically speaking, from Zana's in terms of facial characteristics. Their more sophisticated human features were apparently inherited from their father.

Khwit died at the age of 65 or 70. Fellow villagers described him as being different from his peers. He was reported to be extremely strong, unusually aggressive and generally difficult to deal with – traits that Khwit had in common with the aforesaid Greek hero, Achilles, as described in the archaic legends.

Fig 10 - *The photo above is of Khwit as he appeared in life. The lower photo is of his exhumed skull.*

Before he died, Khwit had moved to the town of T'kvarcheli, but he was returned to T'khina for burial in the Genaba family cemetery.

In September of 1964, the archaeologist V. S. Orelkin made the first attempt to find Zana's gravesite. The Genaba family cemetery, where she was presumably buried, was wildly overgrown. The mound over Khwit's grave was the only location that could be discerned among the underbrush covering the hillside where the cemetery was located. No other burial had taken place since Khwit had been interred ten years before.

Old village residents, and the last descendant of the Genaba clan, seventy-nine-year-old Kenton, were asked about the location of Zana's grave. Kenton was certain that the researchers should dig under a particular pomegranate tree. However, the remains found there turned out to be the corpse of one of Zana's grandchildren who had died early on. The physical profile of this offspring, perceived from the skull, was particularly akin to the profiles of Zana's two living grandchildren who the researchers had previously met.

The researchers had not found Zana's bones, by the second expedition in early 1965 so a third try was undertaken in October of 1965. The group found what they presumed to be the bones of Gamasa. The remains showed slight, but definite, paleoanthropic characteristics.

Three more expeditions to Abkhazia in search of Zana's skeleton were undertaken after Porchnev's passing (I have been unable to verify the date of it). These expeditions took place in 1971, 1975 and 1978. However, by the time of these investigations the last member of the Genaba family had passed away and no one remained who could be reasonably expected to know the location of Zana's gravesite. Thus, the researchers were reported to have never been able to find a skeleton that fit Zana's known traits as described by the eyewitnesses already on the record.

It was finally decided to exhume the skull of Zana's younger son, Khwit, as this was the only grave certain to have a direct connection to her.

Khwit's skull (see photo on next page) was taken to Moscow where it was analyzed by two well-known physical anthropologists, M. A. Kolodieva and M. M. Gerasimova. They reported the results of their study to the Relict Hominoid Research Seminar and the Moscow

Naturalists' Society. These reports were subsequently published in 1987.

Kolodieva compared the skull of Khwit with other male skulls from Abkhazia in the research collection of the Moscow State University Institute of Anthropology. Khwit's skull was judged to be significantly different from these. Kolodieva writes (referring to Khwit's remains as the T'khina skull):

"The Tkhina skull exhibits an original combination of modem and ancient features ... The facial section of the skull is significantly larger in comparison with the mean Abkhaz type ... All the measurements and indices of the superciliary cranial contour are greater not only than those of the mean Abkhaz series, but also than those of maximum size of some fossil skulls studied (or rather were comparable with the latter). The Tkhina skull approaches closest the Neolithic Vovnigi II skulls of the fossil series..."

Gerasimova arrived at the following findings:

"The skull discloses a great deal of peculiarity, a certain disharmony disequilibrium in its features, very large dimensions of the facial skeleton, increased development of the contour of the skull, specificity of the non-metric features (the two foramina mentale in the lower jaw, the intrusive bones in the sagittal suture, and the Inca bone). The skull merits further extended study."

While there are the anecdotal accounts of eyewitnesses to document Zana's extraordinary attributes, there is nothing conclusive, in terms of hard scientific evidence, to confirm her zoological status -- despite the recent study (2009) that examined an exhumed skull, ostensibly Zana's, and found modern human mitochondrial DNA. The identity of the skull, however is hotly contested as there is currently no way to assure that it belonged to Zana.

However, the grounded and specific affirmation of her son's skull does provide support for the testimony of these eyewitnesses making their accounts more credible.

Circuses frequently feature so-called "freaks" as curiosities in their midway exhibits. Many of circus "wildmen" or "wolf boys" turn out to be a simple hoax. A good example is the "Wildman" featured in Waltrer Main's traveling show (see poster image below). Even the great magician, Harry Houdini once played a wildman in a side show. Nevertheless, two circus legends do bear a closer examination.

Clyde Beatty was a renowned circus owner and animal trainer best known for his daring stunts involving wild beasts. According to the "urban legend" I report here, the Beatty Circus, while traveling in Europe in 1925, had somehow procured a Tibetan Yeti that it featured in their exhibits.

This, however, seemed to me to be out of character with Beatty's known preference for African fauna, but is entirely within the character of Beatty's affinity for the extraordinary — given that he was a showman of the Robert Ripley and P.T. Barnum style. It is also entirely possible that the animal reported here was only billed as being a "Tibetan Yeti" when its true genesis was in Africa or even in Europe. (I have already established that similar creatures are known on every continent, and to the circus publicity machine, a wildman is a wildman regardless of its geographic origin. The claim of an exotic source would have only added to its allure and earning potential. But of course, this assumes the animal was not human).

According to the story, when the European tour was over the Circus planned to return to the United States with their newly acquired legendary primate. However, before the Circus could import the animal, the U.S. Customs (or the department responsible for overseeing the import of animals at that time) ostensibly required that the Smithsonian Institution send representatives to examine Beatty's unknown species for disease and confirm the actual zoological status of the creature.

After their examination, the Smithsonian experts ostensibly informed the Beatty Management that the animal could not enter the United States and would have to be released.

The reason they gave to the circus staff was that their "Yeti" was actually a living specimen of H. neandertalensis. At the time the famed John Scopes "Monkey Trial" was taking place in Tennessee. So the impetus for their reasoning was that the media reporting that a living Neanderthal had been captured would have undermined the popular creationist position in favor of Darwin's theory of evolution. In short, such a creature would "prove" Darwin right and the Bible wrong.

Thus, the creature was released back into the wild somewhere in Europe so that it would not to become an "embarrassment" to the American religious community opposed to academic instruction in the concept of Darwinism.

However, and again assuming the animal genuine, I speculate that the issue would have had more to do with the legal ramifications associated with its "human" status than the outcome of the Scopes trial. (If the animal were indeed human, the Beatty organization could have been considered guilty of kidnapping, false imprisonment, human rights violations and so forth if the creature were landed in the United States).

My consultations with the circus museum, circus experts and the

Smithsonian Institute — as well as my friend, Linda Florea, who happens to be the grand niece of William Jennings Brian (a lawyer in the Scopes case) failed to turn up any evidence to support this legend.

There may be some modicum of "truth" in the legend as Beatty did work with Universal Studios in the 1940s on several films featuring Paula the "Ape Woman" as shown in the movie poster above.

In the picture on the right, "Paula" (portrayed by actress Acquanetta) for the movie "Captive Wild Woman" im which "an insane scientist doing experimentation in glandular research becomes obsessed with transforming a female gorilla into a human...even though it costs human life." (according to the plot summary provided for the movie by www.imdb.com).

Thus, it is unlikely that the Beatty

legend is actually true. However, there are wildman legends that appear to hold up to close examination. Encounters with "Wild Men" have been reported in Europe for centuries – although these events are not widely known in the west.

There is a fresco (located on the right), painted in 1464, that depicts one such "Wildman".

The fresco is located in Sacco in val Gerola, Italy on a farm. It shows a hairy, tall man holding a cub and is similar to other European art of the same period. Near the head, there is a caption in Italian that reads: "Ego sonto un homo salvadego per natura, chi me ofende ge fo pagura" which translated into English means: "I am a wildman by nature - I will scare the ones who offend me".

Were this piece of art a single manifestation of the European Bigfoot phenomena, it could easily be dismissed as a hoax or aberration, but there are many other examples of the "Wuderose" or "Woodrose" in European art.

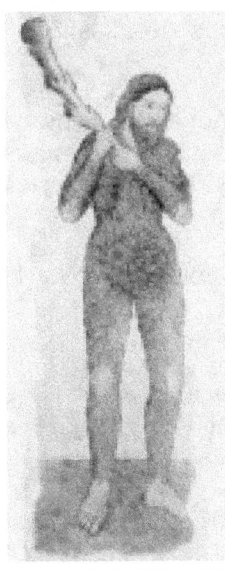

Another Italian wildman fresco located in the Salvàn in Val di Fiemme is associated with a local legend (see image on the left). According to the tradition, many years ago, the peasants of the Mòccheni, saw the depicted creature leaving the forest in Salvàn. They approached it and befriended it. The "wildman" subsequently became a sort of confidant of the townspeople, assisting them in the care of their cattle.

In still another Italian manuscript illumination, (see photo on next page top left) now located among the collections of the Smithsonian Institution in Washington, DC, you'll find an extremely hairy man depicted along with a woman and infant – presumably his wife and off-spring (see illustration next page top left).

This particular artwork more resembles a man with a known medical condition commonly called "The Mexican Wolf Boy Syndrome" than that of a classic (undiscovered animal) Bigfoot.

And, in yet another example of this genre, done in ink on laid paper, is "The Fight in the Forest" appearing lower eft, rendered sometime between 1500 and 1503 by Hans Burgkmair. The piece is currently among the collections of the National Gallery of Art,in Washington, DC where I have had the person priviledge of seeing and holding the artwork itself after requesting a viewing. The work is not currently on display, but is kept archived in a special environment to prevent damage to the piece.

Returing to the carnival circuit for a moment, we should examine the case of Feodor Adrianovitch Jefticheff (AKA Jo Jo the Dog-Face Boy or Wolf Boy) appeared in circus "freak shows" around the world.

Jo Jo, the son of Adrian Maximovitch Jefficheff and Nadia Petrova, was born around the turn of the century (20th) with hair covering his entire body — a condition known as Congenital Generalized Hypertrichosis Lanuginosa.

The condition is hereditary and is often passed on from parent to child — sometimes resulting in hirsute family groups.

Adrian Jefficheff, who also had the affliction, apparently hailed from the area near T'bilisi (Tiflis) in then Russian occupied Georgia. This is interesting in that this general area is in the very same Caucasus Mountain region where Zana was found as discussed previously.

The young Jefficheff (see photo on next page top left) became a colossal business success. In fact, Jo Jo was possibly the most famous wolf

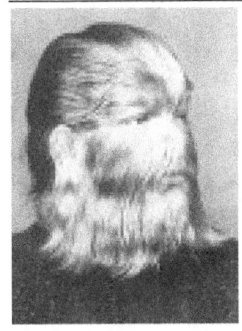

boy attraction in carnival history.

Publicly, Jo Jo only barked and growled as would a wolf, but behind scenes, Jo Jo was fluent in four languages. He was considered to possess a keen intellect by people who were well acquainted with him.

There is some disagreement as to Jo Jo's citizenship. This is probably due to the fact that his agent asserted that Jo Jo was reared by wolves in the Russian forests where hunters had captured him. (Such feral children stories have persisted since before the time of the Roman legends Romulus and Remus) Thus, Jo Jo is often erroneously reported to have been of Russian descent.

A further discussion of the genetic import of these hirsute individuals continues in the Genetic Considerations of Hypertrichosis section of this report.

As mentioned previously, a Swiss geologist, Dr. Francois de Loys and his team conducted an expedition in search of oil reserves around the Rio Tarra and Catatumbo near the Venezuelan and Colombian border in South America from 1917 to 1920. The region around the Sierra de Perijaa is mountainous and was then heavily forested.

While Dr. de Loys and his men were resting on the banks of the Rio Tarra in deep jungle, two large "monkeys" abruptly came out of the woods, screaming and brandishing large sticks at the group.

When the apes threw their excrement at the fearful de Loys and his fatigued crew, the men simply drew their guns and fired at the more aggressive male, but their shots killed the female.

The male primate, although wounded, disappeared into the forest.

In analyzing de Loys' account, I am struck by the congruity of the described behavior of his "monkeys" with that of chimpanzees and lowland gorillas. The vocalizations and arm waving are consistent with known great ape behavior, as is the action of flinging dung at a perceived threat.

I am also fascinated by the apparent tool use (the sticks) – not to be

Fig. 12 - *Francois de Loys' photo of his "monkey." Note that a tail is not evident in the photograph. Thus the primate is an ape and not a monkey.*

confused with tool making. Tool use is a behavior well documented by Jane Goodall's anthropological studies of chimpanzees. Although still controversial, tool use by at least one lowland gorilla has been reported.[2] Most sightings of Bigfoot creatures do not indicate that the animal carried or used tools during an encounter with the notable exception being Bigfoot creatures in Europe and Asia.

Neither chimps, nor lowland gorilla range in South America and it is unlikely that any would have escaped from a nearby zoo or have been someone's exotic pet at this time and in this locale. Thus, de Loys' encounter can not easily be dismissed as a known animal out of place.

More compelling is that Dr. de Loys had the presence of mind and the scientific training to make a proper record of the female primate's body on film and retained the snapshot in his journal with the entry of the encounter and some physical attribute measurements of the animal.

Actually, it was the French anthropologist, Georges Montandon, who discovered de Loys' photo as he, sometime later, flipped through the pages of de Loys' journal only then recognizing the real significance of the animal.

Montandon was familiar with the primates that had been discovered up to that time but had never seen one that looked anything like de Loys' "Monkey". Montandon realized that the large primate in the picture had very human-like characteristics — in addition to the fact that it had no tail. Its height, according to de Loys' record, was 4 feet 5 inches. The ape had 32 teeth. It had all the features that qualified it as an anthropoid ape – not a monkey.

The so-called "de Loy's Ape" was classified as Ameranthropoides loysi in 1929. The Motilone Indians of the region readily identified the creature as their Mono Rei – a species of legendary South American Wildman or Bigfoot.

Unfortunately, leading anthropologists of the day discounted de Loys' find and attributed his alleged "monkey" attack to the spectacled bear (Tremarctos ornatus). This is unlikely as the body length of the adult ornatus is about 150 to 180 centimeters (60 to 72 inches) and males may be 30 to 40 percent larger than females. Males weigh 100 to 155 kilograms (220 t o 340 pounds) and females weigh 64 to 82 kilograms (140 to 180 pounds). Although the spectacled bear does have a snout that is shorter than most bear species, the animal does not resemble the creature in the photograph taken by de Loys.

Further confusing the scientific community was Marquis de Wavrin's assertion that de Loys' creatures were actually spider monkeys (Ateles belzebuth). However the spider monkey typically attains a head and body length of about 2 feet and has a pronounced tail that can be up to an additional 3 feet in length. The animal's weight is 13 to17 pounds. Again, this animal does not fit the profile of de Loys ape – if only because the spider monkey has a prehensile tail, which is conspicuously lacking in the de Loys creature.

Nevertheless, Montandon's interpretation of the de Loys ape was discredited — until recently. Fortunately, de Loys' photograph survives and, in the light of today's zoological knowledge, has led to more comprehensive investigations into his "man-ape" that appears to be roaming the South American jungles.

The recently "discovered" Bili Ape (or the "N'goloko" Bigfoot as it is locally known) was

Fig. 13 - *The Spectacled Bear, or Tremarctos ornatus, appears in the top image while the Spider Monkey (Ateles belzebuth) is shown in the lower photo.*

Neither of these animals is close in appearance to the de Loys' ape shown on the previous page.

actually rumored to exist for nearly 100 years prior it its scientific "confirmation" in 2004. This animal was originally thought to be a pongid that shares certain characteristics with simioids. This originally suggested that the animal was an entirely new species rather than a sub-species of pongid, but this isn't the case.

The Bili (or Bondo) Ape (see photo on the left) is reportedly larger in size than the lowland gorilla and ranges near the Uele River in the northern Republic of the Congo's Bondo swamp area. This location is a considerable distance from the known range of the mountain gorilla and the established habitat of the Lowland gorilla.[3]

DNA tests on fecal samples from the Bili Ape have been determined by Omaha's Henry Doorly Zoo and have determined that the animal is a sub-species of chimpanzee, *Pan troglodytes schweinfurthii*.

Many researchers are quick to point out that Bigfoot legends go back hundreds of years. I have already mentioned European accounts that extend back to the 13th century, but I should also clarify that stories of Bigfoot-like animals actually extend back thousands of years – not just a few centuries.

The Epic of Gilgamesh, the oldest written story known, comes to us from ancient Sumeria. Considered one of the earliest civilizations, Sumeria was composed of city-states located around the lower Tigris and Euphrates rivers in what is today southern Iraq.

The Gilgamesh Epic was originally inscribed on 12 clay tablets in cuneiform script. The story chronicles the adventures of a historical King of Uruk and takes place somewhere between 2750 and 2500 BCE.

In the Epic, Enkidu is described as a wild-man reared by animals. Enkidu's description is identical to that of Bigfoot animals reported today. In the story, Enkidu is "tamed" by a female courtesan of the court of Gilgamesh named "Shamhat". He becomes a friend of the story's central hero and has adventures with him until his death. This translation of the ancient account of a Bigfoot (Enkidu) is described in Tablet I of the Epic (see photo right). Translation below:

When Aruru heard this she created within herself the zikrtt of Anu.

Aruru washed her hands, she pinched off some clay, and threw it into the wilderness.

In the wildness(?) she created valiant Enkidu, born of Silence, endowed with strength by Ninurta.

His whole body was shaggy with hair, he had a full head of hair like a woman, his locks billowed in profusion like Ashnan.

He knew neither people nor settled living, but wore a garment like Sumukan.

He ate grasses with the gazelles, and jostled at the watering hole with the animals; as with animals, his thirst was slaked with (mere) water.

A notorious trapper came face-to-face with him opposite the watering hole.

A first, a second, and a third day he came face-to-face with him opposite the watering hole.

On seeing him the trapper's face went stark with fear, and he (Enkidu?) and his animals drew back home.

He was rigid with fear; though stock-still his heart pounded and his face drained of color.

Some older versions of the Epic transliterate Enkidu's name as "Enkimdu", "Eabani" or "Enkita".

The Epic of Gilgamesh pre-dates the Judeo-Christian bible and is considered the source of the biblical account of Noah and the Flood (which also is mentioned in the context of the adventures). This ancient account is the oldest written record in which a Bigfoot-like animal or person is described that has been found to date.

Fig. 14 - *Gilgamesh (wrestling with a lion) pictured with Enkidu (riding a bull) in this cylinder seal impression from excavations in Ur located in today's Iraq. the cuneiform script on the right is the oldest type of 'pictographic' writing known for this culture.*

Attributing accounts of Bigfoot animals to the status of a contemporary hoax becomes difficult to justify as the historical evidence I've described here would require that the scope and profundity of the "joke" extend, not only beyond simple geographical borders, but over millennia of time.

So, while contemporary hoaxters have interjected a complicating element into proper scientific Bigfoot investigations, there is a significant, and credible, body of evidence supporting the notion that there is some sort of unidentified or unexplained bipedal hairy primate or primate-like animal roaming around the planet.

In light that reports of these animals have been with us for millennia, to conclude that Bigfoot can be dismissed as simply some sort of conspiracy, perpetrated for reasons unknown, by some covert society over thousands of years, or some sort of mass hysteria becomes utter nonsense. Clearly, there must be more to the story than a few contemporary headlines and the frauds perpetrated on the media and on film by modern pranksters.

The answer to the Bigfoot mystery must then be far more complex than a superficial application of Occam's Razor would otherwise suggest.

The Fossil Record

One of the principal criticisms that taint the possible existence of Bigfoot-like creatures is that their remains are not found in the fossil record. Point-in-fact, this assertion is likely to be inaccurate.

Certain of these creatures are conceivably species thought to be extinct. I have already enumerated at least two accounts where the ostensibly extinct Neanderthal was cited as the creature associated with those Bigfoot interactions. It is conceivable that other members of the Hominin family line could still exist as well.

Another possible creature responsible for Bigfoot sightings is the obscure hominid species Meganthropus; the fossil remains of which are known to science. The newly identified species Homo antecessor (from the Latin for pioneer or explorer) is now thought to be the direct ancestor to both modern H. sapiens and H. neandertalensis. This new human species was found at Gran Dolina, a railway cut in northern Spain's Sierra Atapuerca.

The newly discovered Pierolapithecus catalaunicus, also found in Spain (near Barcelona) in 2004, lived about 13 million years ago. The animal is a probable common ancestor to great apes and thus humans. It had a body similar to apes, fingers like a chimpanzee and apparently had the upright posture of humans.

Other, the pongid species like Gigantopithicus (as proposed by Dr. Grover Krantz) is also considered by some to be a feasible as antecessor of some of the larger of the Bigfoot-like creatures – if not Bigfoot itself. It too is already known to science.

The recent discovery of the dwarf species Homo florensiensis in Southeast Asia suggests that the legends of diminutive Bigfoot-like animals, specifically the Ebu Gogo, inhabiting the islands and forests of this region may, indeed, have some basis in fact.[4]

So, the discoveries of Hominid relatives such as Homo antecessor, Pierolapithecus catalaunicus and Australopithecus garhi suggest that there are, or were, more hominid species that roam(ed) the planet than previously thought. The discovery of H florensiensis, thought to be a diminutive variation of H. erectus, (I disagree and believe it to be a species in its own right) presumed to have gone extinct 400,000 years ago, introduces another exception to the mainstream science extinction pronouncement doctrine.

The survival of H. florensiensis into the last ice age strongly suggests that H. Sapiens may not be the only surviving member of the genus Homo on the planet.

Thefore it would seem to be non-sequitur that we presume that only one member of our genus survives today when most other animal life on the planet embraces more than one species in a given genus.

Ramapithecus, (see illustration above) another extinct primate that lived from about 12 to 14 million years ago, could also have engendered progeny that account for some Bigfoot "species." Formerly regarded as an ancestor of Australopithecus, and therefore of humans, fossil remains of Ramapithecus (now called *Sivapithecus)* were discovered in Northern India and in Eastern Africa beginning in 1932.

Although obviously an apelike creature, Ramapithecus was originally considered a human ancestor solely on the basis of reconstructed jaw and dental attributes derived from fragmentary fossils. Subsequently, a complete jaw was discovered in 1976, which was determined to be non-hominid. Ramapithecus is now regarded as a predecessor of today's orangutan.

It would seem at least possible that, the doctrinal assertion that all these creatures no longer existent may be in error (a generality erratum that is replete in the annals of science) and the statement that Bigfoot is not supported by fossil evidence is subject to contention.

I will speak more on this later, but for now, I'd like to review what fossils are and how they form.

The Fossilization Process and Fossil Types

Lay people often get confused when professionals talk about the "fossil record." This is because they are typically familiar with only one type of fossil – those that have been *permineralized* – the type they usually see at museums of dinosaur skeletons and those of other megafauna. (Actually, these "remains" are often fiberglass or resin reproductions of the real fossil).

However, the actual scope of material types that consititute fossils to a scientist is much broader than that. Certain details about any fossil find in the field includes the way in which the remains are preserved. That information indicates the method of preservation the happened to the organism's remains subsequent to its death, and the conditions under which the fossil material was created.

Indeed, most organic remains do not become fossilized after the organism's death. All organic material begins to decay after an organism dies and will decompose entirely over time. In the wild, a more immediate issue is that animal carcasses are often subjected to predation and scavenging which leaves incomplete and disarticulated fossil specimens that are found at a later time.

There are essentially two principle fossil types:

▶ **Body Fossils** which are the preserved remains of an organism's body tissue, or parts thereof, that have become fossilized in an altered or actual state, and

▶ **Trace Fossils** which constitute any evidence left behind by an organism that is not tissue remains. Examples of trace fossils are animal tracks, trails, burrows borings, impressions, molds, casts, and steinkerns.

But, there are a number of ways in which these fossils type are preserved. To become fossilized, tissue has to be subjected to particular environmental conditions that are conducive to the specific manner of preservation.

Unless an organism happens to die in anaerobic environment, its soft parts will not be preserved. For this reason, fossilization of "soft tissue," such as muscles, skin, and organs, are unusual.

Generally speaking, the important circumstance to fossilization is rapid burial and the existence of "hard tissue' components like bones and teeth in the remains. If an organism is not quickly buried, microbes and other animals will devour the remains. Large predators and scavengers often gnaw or smash bone for its marrow content and the material will be lost to the fossil record. Even if remains do become fossilized, natural erosion processes can destroy them over time.

There are actually quite a few ways in which organic tissue can become a fossil. These are classified as:

Unaltered Preservation refers to fossils that have undergone little or no change in structure and composition. A fossil of an organism that lived recently is more likely to be unaltered than a more aged one.

Original Skeletal Material refers to the hard tissues that are preserved as the original ekoskeleton or casing enclosing the animal's soft tissues. This includes many invertebrate molluska that have shells composed of calcium carbonate, silica, or chitin and vertebrate species with bones composed of calcium phosphate.

Encrustations occur in caves where ground water with a high concentration of dissolved minerals seeps or drips constantly. As the water evaporates, the minerals are remain. These chemicals then form a thin coating on the interior surface of the cave and remains that lie in it thereby preserving organisms that die there.

Tar Impregnation is excellent for fossilization. The La Brea tar pits of California yield particularly fine collections of vertebrate bones, wood, and so forth. Smaller tar pits frequently yield perfectly preserved insects and their larvae.

In **Amber Entombment** coniferous trees, like spruce, pine and fir, that have a sticky resinous pitch that seeps from damage to the tree's bark. Many small insects and other small organisms occasionally become trapped in the resin. After burial the sap hardens into amber. Particular areas of the Baltic Sea coastline and a few islands in the West Indies are well known for insects preserved in amber.

Refrigeration primarily occured during the Pleistocene Era, when ice sheets covered much of the Northern Hemisphere. During this periodt, some animals fell into crevasses or became trapped in permanently frozen soil or ice. Although infrequent, some have been discovered perfectly preserved in this manner.

Mummification occurs in very arid environments. The animal's remains dehydrate or desiccate quickly and become preserved — usually including its soft tissues.

As sediment layers become compressed by the weight of overlying material, they slowly undergo the process of lithification. It is common for cementing materials in the groundwater like carbonate, silica, and iron oxides, to bond the sediment together and harden. Often the groundwater, and the minerals contained in it, impacts the fossilization process.

In **Permineralization**, bones, teeth, carteledge and plant matter have porous internal structures. These pores become filled with mineral deposits in the soil and groundwater. In the process of permineralization, the actual chemical composition of the original hard parts of the organism may not change but it generally will be altered in some way producing a rock-like replica of the actual tissue.

Carbonization occurs when an organism becomes pressed into sediment and its volatile, liquid or gaseous contents are forced out leaving a thin film of carbon. When other organic material remains, as when plants are entombed, coal is formed. Thus, coal mines are typically a good source for carbonized fossils.

In *Recrystallization* the hard tissues are converted, usually in a solid state, into a new mineral or to coarser crystals of than those of the original mineral.

Compression refers to fossils that form as a result of pressure from sediments that cover an organism or trace fossils of it. Compression usually is used to describe the casts and/or molds of plant leaves.

Dissolution or *Replacement* refers to fossils formed when groundwater, particularly if it is acidic, acts upon the remains to dissolve the hard and soft tissue structures of an organism trapped in sediments. The hard tissues are often simultaneously replaced by minerals contained in the water — molecule by molecule. Petrified wood is a classic example of this type of fossilization where even the internal microscopic cellular structure of the plant is replaced by silica in the process of fossilization.

Authingenic Preservation occurs when a mold or form of an organism is made after it decomposes in sediment and is replaced by material that hardens into a casting of the original animal's likeness. Animals with exoskeletons or shells are often fossilized in this way. Fossils of animals with shells, particularly molluska, are sometimes called *Steinkerns*.

A *Mold* refers to any reproduction of an organism's past presence in the environment that has been preserved by leaving an impression, but not necessarily filled with hardened material such as an animal's track or footprint.

Generally speaking, a *Cast* is any copy of the original mold form when the "positive" item is removed or dissolved away and the remaining "negative" impression becomes filled with sediment or mineral material that subsequently hardens into a replica of the original.

Borings and *Burrows* from when worms, clams and other burrowing invertebrates "drill" into rocks, wood, shells, and all types of sediment. These cavities are frequently preserved, especially in fine-grained rocks and may also appear in the bones of vertebrate animals.

Coprolite is the fossilized excrement from a animal and is sometimes very useful in providing knowledge about specific diet of the animal concerned.

Gastroliths are smooth, polished stones that are typically found in the abdominal cavities of skeletal fossils of dinosaurs and large mammals. These "grinding stones" are thought to have been essential for the animal's digestion of plant material by grinding up vegetable matter in their stomach.

Gnawings are the result of rodent, marsupial and other animals that chewed on bones or trees.

Unaltered preservation usually involves insects or plant parts that become trapped in amber, a form of tree sap that hardens with the animal or plant preserved inside.

Butchering generally refers to fossil bones which bear scratches or markings that indicate the cutting away of tissue with a sharp implement. Fossils of this sort, due to the use of tools in the cutting process, indicate the presence and interaction of a tool-using animal like man at the time of the organism's death.

We will see and discuss some of these fossil types in the following sections of this report detailing pertinent aspects of physical evidence of Bigfoot creatures as they relate to fossilized preservation.

But, as you can see, many of the fossilization processes require that highly specialized environmental conditions exist in the location of the process. For example, water and the proper minerals must be present for permineralization to occur.

Since only a very small percentage of the animal life that ever existed will be found in fossil form, it follows that the probability that a naturally rare animal like a Bigfoot would be found in a fossilized state becomes even more remote.

Nevertheless, there is evidence of some primitive primates evolving in North America in the scant but verified fossil record. One of the reasons that there aren't prolific fossil remains to trace the development of primates on the North American continent is the glaciation that occurred during the ice age which disrupted and pulverized the geological layers in which these remains would have otherwise been found on much of the continent.

Preserved Specimens

The confirmation of the N'goloko's (Bili Ape) existence by contemporary science in 2004 belies the fact that the animal's skeletal remains had been sitting on a shelf at the Congo Museum in Tervueren since 1898.

In fact, a curator of the museum, Henri Schouteden, was sufficiently struck by the anatomical differences from known gorilla skulls that he dubbed the primate a sub-species *Gorilla gorilla uellensis* before Dr. Colin Groves (mistakenly) dismissed the remains as "indistinguishable" from the western lowland gorilla in 1970.

Grove's apparently cavalier pronouncement is fascinating in the light of the prevailing rush, among physical anthropologists, to christen a new species of hominid in the fossil record in spite of known conditions that could render anomalous fossil finds a simple variation or aberration on a previously established hominid species.

In the early 1960s a man by the name of Frank Hansen obtained the "Ice Mummy" of some sort of hominid creature frozen within a block of ice (see photo below). Hansen's own account, which appeared in Saga Magazine in 1970, regarding his acquisition of the Iceman is that he shot it while hunting in the backwoods of Minnesota. In another account a women named Helen Westring ostensibly shot the creature when it attacked her.

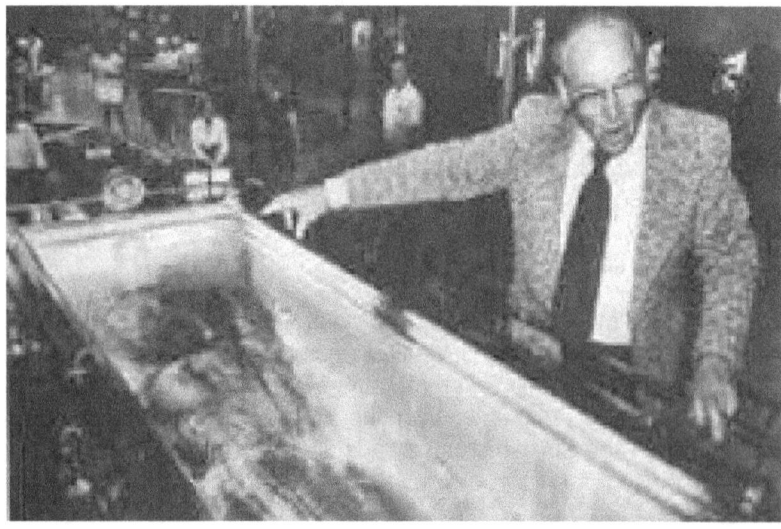

Actually, both stories are likely fabrications. Dr. Helmut Loofs-Wissowa of the Australian National University believed that the specimen actually came from Vietnam and was smuggled into the United States by Hansen. Thus, Hansen's "Iceman" could have been a specimen of a Vietnamese Bigfoot known as the "Nguoi Rung".

This assertion makes sense in that Hansen was a Vietnam air force veteran and had returned from service to the United States a short time before he began touring the United States with his "Minnesota Iceman" exhibit at various carnivals, exhibit halls and public gathering places.

Terry Cullins, now a Doctor of zoology, went to view the Iceman in 1968 when he was 17 years of age. Actually, Cullins was so fascinated with the exhibit that he returned several times — even taking a magnifying glass to examine the oddity more closely.

The "Nguoi Rung" of Vietnam

Cullins says that the creature appeared to be an adolescent male about 6 feet tall. The corpse had a death grimace on his face and appeared to have had a severe injury to one side of his face. Cullins said he could clearly make out all four incisor teeth though the ice, which he said had similarity to those of an orangutan. More importantly, young Cullins was certain that he was looking at a "Missing Link" in human evolution.

After trying unsuccessfully to get scientists to come and confirm his appraisal of the creature, Cullins could coax only one anthropologist from the University of Minnesota to look the thing over.

The anthropologist examined the corpse for about ten minutes and then silently walked away. Collins, highly frustrated, contacted two men: Ivan T. Sanderson, a naturalist and well-known author, and Dr. Bernard Heuvelmans, the acknowledged "Father of Cryptozoology."

Heuvelmans and Sanderson went to see Hansen's Iceman at Cullins' urging. After a second visit, Sanderson was able to scrape away some of the ice in a section of the block where the creature was more accessible. Sanderson said he could smell the putrefaction from the flesh. He also discovered that the Iceman had been shot through the eye and had a broken arm.

Now convinced that Iceman was genuine, Heuvelmans and Sanderson wrote an article published in Argosy magazine in May of 1969 called, "Living Fossil".

Subsequently, the pair went to the local sheriff to inform him of their findings. Shortly thereafter, the FBI and Smithsonian Institution took an interest in the Iceman.

As a result of the official inquiries, and Heuvelman and Sanderson's statements, the sheriff paid a visit to Hansen to inform him that he may have broken several laws — if Sanderson and Heuvelman were correct in their appraisal of his exhibit.

The sheriff intended to bring a pathologist from the Smithsonian out to the Hansen home the next morning to verify Sanderson and Heuvelman's finding. However, Hansen vanished with his "Iceman" only to return to the county fair and carnival circuits with an obvious replica of the original exhibit months later.

The whereabouts of the actual "Iceman" remains unknown to this day.

Creatures frozen in ice, as opposed to permineralized remains, are not nearly so common. Mammoth remains have been recovered from blocks of ice having been quick-frozen, as it were, during some climatic event or after an apparent fall into a large ice cold water source. Other prehistoric animals have been similarly discovered. But, prehistoric human remains preserved in this way are rare.

Nevertheless, In 1991, a Neolithic Homo sapien specimen was found, frozen in ice, near Hauslabjoch in the Ötzal Alps. This "Iceman" was retrieved from the ice pack and subsequently examined by European scientists. So, the format of Hansen's Iceman acquisition, as reported by Cullins, Sanderson and Heuvelmans, shouldn't be considered improbable.

While the forensic examination of these "Ice Mummies" can tell us a great deal about their zoological status, physical health, life and culture, science needs the actual specimen to make these determinations in a laboratory.

So, until the actual Minnesota Iceman is recovered, we have only Sanderson, Heuvelman, and Cullins accounts to rely on.

In 1941 a Russian combat unit fighting the Germans in the Caucasus Mountains near Buinakst was asked by a resistance group to take a look at an unusual prisoner they had taken.

According to Lt. Col. Vargen Karapetyan, the Russian unit's commander, the captive was a naked, hairy man that was covered with body lice.

This is interesting because lice are very particular parasites which are specialized to particular host species and only feed on certain areas of the host's body. Since the louse's life cycle is spent entirely with its host (after initial infestation) lice have developed special adaptations that enable them to exist in a certain "habitat" found on the host. These adaptations can be evident in the size (from 0.5 mm to 8 mm) of the louse, its appendages, and claws, which are adapted to cling tightly to body hair, fur or feathers

Body lice (*Pediculus humanus corporis*) are specific to humans and and generally seen more often in underdeveloped countries. They are typically associated with poverty, overcrowding, and poor hygiene — conditions that one would expect in the case of an Almasty or Kaptar, the Russian version of a Bigfoot.

According to the story, the prisoner could not understand speech and appeared to be moronic. He blinked his eyes often and was obviously afraid, but made no attempt to defend himself, even when Karapetyan pulled some hairs from its body.

The prisoner was kept in a barn, because he emitted a noxious odor and dripped sweat when he was imprisoned in a heated room. Obviously unusual for a Homo sapiens, but perhaps not for a Homo neanderthalensis — the hominin that Russian scientists attribute as their Bigfoot animal.

Seeing no need to become involved in this affair, Karapetyan instructed the partisans to do what they deemed appropriate with their captive.

Some accounts say that the creature later escaped or was let go, but according to a report made by the Ministry of the Interior filed sometime later in Daghestan, the 'wildman' had been executed as a deserter after being duly court-martialed.

In a more contemporary account, a worker at an experimental agricultural station operated by the Mongolian Academy of Sciences at Bulgan in 1980, encountered the dead body of a Bigfoot (Almas/ Almasty):

"I approached and saw a hairy corpse of a robust humanlike creature dried and half-buried by sand. I had never seen such a humanlike being before covered by camel-color brownish-yellow short hairs and I recoiled, although in my native land in Sinkiang I had seen many dead men killed in battle. ... The dead thing was not a bear or ape and at the same time it was not a man like Mongol or Kazakh or Chinese and Russian. The hairs of its head were longer than on its body" (Shackley 1983, p. 107).

If only this desert mummy had been recovered, examined and preserved! What tales would it have told to modern science?

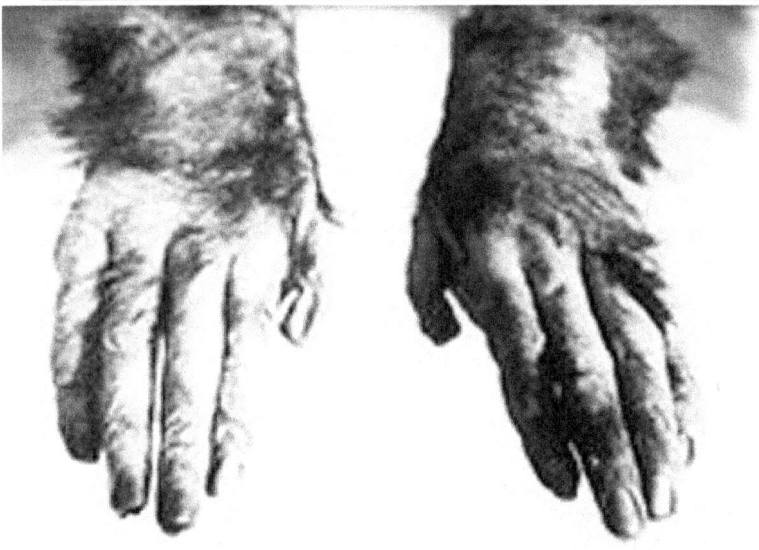

Fig. 15 - *A pair of "Yeti Hands" found in China, mummified and preservced. The long fingers and anatomy suggest a primate as the source. But no tests have been done to confirm that they are anything other than Gibbon.*

Primate Evolution

It seems appropriate to discuss the development of primates at this juncture. Specifically: How could there be unknown primates on the North and South American and Australian continents when conventional theories state that hominid primates came out of Africa?

Primates, as a group are fairly recent creatures on this planet. The prosimian primogenitors of primates evolved after about 70 percent all species of animal had ostensibly become extinct at the end of the age of dinosaurs as a result of events set in motion by the collision of a meteor or comet with the Earth.

Earth is estimated to be about 4.5 billion years old. Life forms began to emerge about 3.5 billion years ago. Transitional mammilla began to develop near the end of the Mesozoic Era about 65 million years ago. The first primates didn't come on the scene until around 60 million years ago.

Sixty million years ago the world was very different place. The continents, as we now know them, were in different locations than they are today. North America was still directly connected to Europe. South America had drifted away from Africa, but had not yet collided with the North American continent. India was not conjoined with Asia and Australia was just a hop from Antarctica.

The landmasses, as a rule, enjoyed a warm tropical or subtropical climate that supported lush, rain forests. The flowering, grassland plains remained millennia away from developing.

Large reptiles were in the process of being replaced by the mammals as the new, dominant large land animals. At first, there were a few archaic land mammals like the monotremes (egg-layer ancestors of the platypus and echidna). The few placental mammals existing at the time were mainly Insectivore predecessors of the primates. Marsupials – raccoon-like, pouched mammals existed in somewhat larger numbers. The large herbivore placental mammals like bovines didn't yet exist as the immense grasslands they would need for a food resource did not yet exist. At the time, rodents and small-seed eating birds had not yet evolved for similar reasons.

The firt proto-primates, were approximately akin to the tree shrews and squirrels we are familiar with today in size and appearance. The fossil evidence (much of it admittedly from Africa) strongly suggests that they were arboreal and preferred a moist climate. It's likely they had good eyesight as well as paws with footpads and claws for climbing.

It appears that these early primate-like mammals didn't have a particularly important role to play in the comprehensive transmogrification of animal life taking place on dry land during this period.

More dramatic changes came about with the emergence of the large grazing and browsing mammals with tough hoofs, grinding teeth, and digestive tracts specialized for the processing of grass, leaves, and other fibrous plant materials of the grassy plains.

With the advance of the plant-eaters, the meat-eating predators and scavengers like canines, felines, and ursids could evolve. Adaptive

Fig. 16 - *Smilodectes - an extinct genus of proto-primate that lived in Wyoming, USA. It was one of the handful of extremely primitive primates that inhabited North America along with its better known cousin Notharctus.*

radiation resulted in the emergence of new species that could fill the expanding ecological niches left by the dinosaurs and the opportunities brought about by climatic shifts and the resultant new flora and low on the food-chain fauna.

Primates first appeared during the last part of the Paleocene Epoch. Their fossils have been found in 60 million year-old geological deposits of Morocco. Some early paleontologists postulated that primates also developed on continents as well as Africa and Asia. Indeed, primate fossil finds from North America are now known to include Smilodectes (see illustration above), Rooneyia omomyid, and Notharctus. If you a dd to these recent early primate fossil finds from Utah (now being prepared for display by Dr. Jonathan Bloch at the Florida Natural History Museum), there is ample evidence that confirms their assertions.

This is a significant issue that is very germane to this report.

The early Eocene Epoch corresponds with the emergence of many of the contemporary placental mammal classifications. Among these are primate species that resemble modern prosimians like the lemurs, lorises, and possibly the tarsiers and galagos of today. Point of fact, the Eocene was a time of maximum prosimian adaptive radiation in evolutionary terms. There were about 60 genera of prosimians that were mostly organized in two families — the Adapidae, like the lemurs and lorises, and the Omomyidae, like galagos and tarsiers. And, as you I have already related, Eocene prosimians are now known to have lived in North America, Europe, Africa, and Asia.

From an evolutionary point of view, the brains and eyes of these prosimians became larger. Their snouts got smaller. But, there is something else that had to happen to pave the way for bipeds.

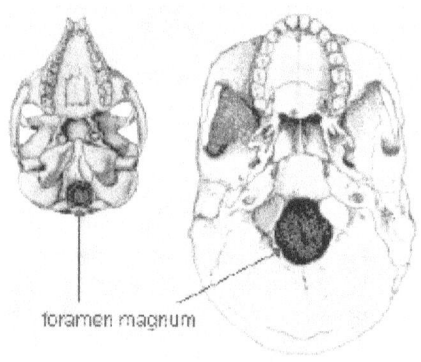

There is a hollow at the base of the skull called the *Foramen Magnum* through which the spinal cord passes to the brain. The location of this hole is a

foramen magnum

cogent indicator of the angle of the spinal column relative to the head. If it is set back, the animal would be oriented horizontally like a quadruped. If it is centered, the animal's body becomes oriented vertically like a biped.

The foramen magnum in select primate species began to move from the back of the skull towards its center during the Eocene. The implication of this is that these prosimians were beginning to stand erect while hopping and sitting like the modern lemurs, galagos, and tarsiers do today. This is a significant development in primates in that it was the essential physiological change required for upright posture common to all hominids.

By the start of the Oligocene Epoch, North America and Europe had broken apart and became distinct continents. The Great Rift Valley of Eastern Africa formed during the Oligocene along the 1,200-mile, volcanically active fault zone between large tectonic sections of the African plate.

The Indian sub-continent collided with southern Asia during the Eocene Epoch, about 55 million years ago. This tetonic activity forced up the Himalayas and the Tibetan Plateau changing the worldwide weather patterns that gave the post-dinosaur world its generally moderate climate by blocking the summer monsoonal rains that the rain-forested world depended upon.

Monkey species evolved as branch off of the prosimian line during the Oligocene — perhaps a bit earlier. The well-known Apidium was approximately the size of a chubby squirrel at 2 to 3 pounds. Its larger cousin, the Aegyptopithecus was the size of a large domestic cat weighing 13 to 20 pounds. Both were arboreal herbivores that apparently ate fruit and seeds.

Compared to the earlier prosimians, these primitive monkeys had fewer teeth, less elongated fox-like snouts (a point also important to this paper), larger brains, and the increasingly more forward-looking eyes that are essential to stereoscopic vision.

It is assumed, by paleontologists, that the scarcity of Oligocene Epoch prosimian fossils indicates that monkeys competed with, and replaced, their prosimian antecedents in most environments. This idea is supported by the fact that modern prosimians live in locations where monkeys and apes are absent from the local fauna or they are nocturnal and thus don't present a threat to the more intelligent daylight functioning primates. But, this may not have been the case in all geographic areas in which primates evolved.

The significant geological changes and consequent regional climate shifts during the Oligocene Epoch impacted evolution and undoubtedly altered the fossil preservation conditions in many areas as outlined previously.

A cooling and drying trend that began in the late Eocene Epoch accelerated, especially in the Northern Hemisphere. One result was the widespread disappearance of early primates from the northern latitudes. However, this is not to say that some species of these early primates did not adapt to the cooler, but still warmer, temperatures than we have today, or that they couldn't migrate into regions with a more moderate type of climate.

Growing polar ice caps reduced the amount of water in the oceans, causing sea levels to drop. This exposed previously submerged coastal lands to habitation. The land bridge between Africa and Asia re-emerged to provide a migration route for primates and other animals between these continents. Woodland hammocks and dry grasslands replaced east African and South Asian tropical rain forest. These environmental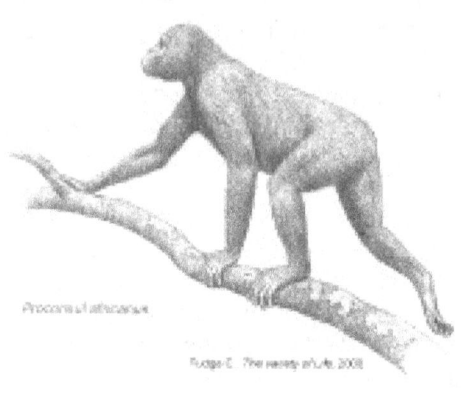

Proconsul africanus

changes are though to have brought about adaptations that apparently impacted primate evolution. It is also likely that these sea level changes obliterated much of the fossil record that could shed more light on primate development along coastal areas that occurred this time.

Apes evolved from monkeys early in the Miocene Epoch. Fossil monkey and prosimian remains are comparatively rare during most of the Miocene, but apes, like the Proconsul, were fairly common. Thus, it would seem that apes of the Miocene occupied many of the same ecological niches that would later be occupied by monkeys.

The Miocene primates included the ancestors of all modern ape and human species. By 14 million years ago, the group of apes that, according to current theory, included our immediate ancestors, were engaged in the process of adapting to life on the edges of the expanding grassland savannas in Southern Europe. By the end of the Miocene, cooler conditions in the Northern Hemisphere apparently caused most primate species to become extremely scarce or extinct. Some of these species appear to have endured by migrating south to more temperate areas and it seems that some may have survived by adapting to an aquatic environment.

TIMELINE OF PRIMATE EVOLUTION

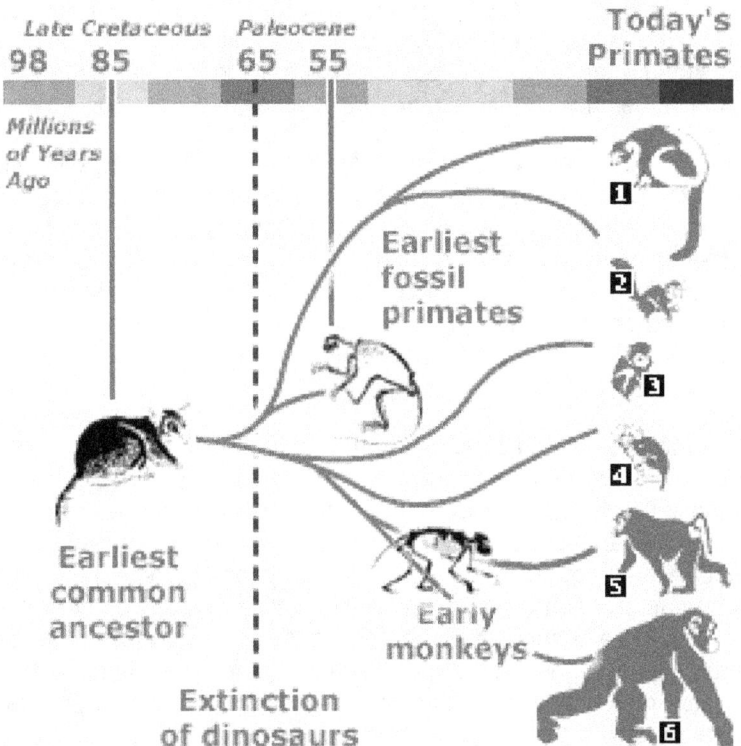

Around 9 million years ago, the descendants of Dryopithecines the anthropoid ape ancestor in Africa branched into two groups — gorillas and simians. Approximately 3 million years later, another split occurred in the simian lineage that branched into the chimpanzees and hominids.

Early prosimian primates emerged during the Paleocene, 65 to 54 Million years ago (at which time North America had not yet separated from Europe). Apes first appeared on the scene during the Eocene, 54 to 33 million years ago. The first hominins evolved during the Pliocene, 5.3 to 1.8 million years ago – according to the fossil record established in Africa and Asia.

The North American conditions weren't conducive to the preservation of fossilized remains during the Pliocene and beyond in the Northern areas of the continent as a series of ice ages took place at nearly the same time that these primates would have been evolving – assuming parallel development with their Asian and African counterparts. Those primate species that migrated south towards today's Gulf Coast would have lived in areas that are now under water as the coastline of the day was not at its present location due to lower sea levels resulting from the ice pack taking up more of the planet's water supply.

The ice sheet that impacted much of North America covered Canada and extended into the great plains of the United States almost to Saint Louis, Missouri. The glacier itself would have effectively erased any evidence of primates in these northern great plains regions and those that survived would have had to migrate to the more temperate area along the coast of the Gulf of Mexico. However, the coastal plain during the Ice Ages was farther out from the present shoreline – approximately 80 miles farther into the waters of the present-day Gulf.

In South America these New World primates probably continued to evolve into forms that are similar, but not necessarily identical, to those found in Africa, Asia and Europe. Some of these forms likely returned to North America, along with other South American species like the peccary and jaguarundi, around 3 million years ago when the South American and North American tetonic plates joined and the climate became more hospitable. Of course, as the sea levels rose at the end of the ice age, the ocean waters covered the fossil evidence of these coastal treks between continents that had taken place thousands of years before.

Mainstream science holds to the idea that contemporary hominids evolved only in African grassland. Mitochondrial DNA evidence tends to support this contention but is not conclusive. So we cannot be certain that all primate species followed this developmental convention. Since it is evident that primates did evolve on multiple continents, and that evolutionary dynamics resultant of the varied geography may not have followed identical paths, it is feasible that some of their progeny survived to become the Bigfoot creatures that are the point of this report.

It is possible that some legendary biped primates possessing more aquatic characteristics are the result of an adaptation to alternate environmental conditions.

Prosimian, pongid and simian species have never been particularly prolific when compared to creatures that are lower on the food chain. Even early hominin species were not abundant, until the advent of H. sapiens. Essentially, most hominid anthropoids have existed as "an endangered species" ever since they first evolved.

So dismissing Bigfoot and his cousins casually, simply because of scarcity or failure to follow dogmatic evolutionary paths, isn't supported by the established standards of the primate family. Indeed, the recently confirmed existence of the N'goloko or Bili Ape and the apparent existence, as evidenced by photography, of the Mono Rei or de Loys' Ape would appear to add weight to this point.

Moreover, assuming that hominin species, other than those tracing their lineage back to Africa, all came to an evolutionary dead end contradicts the innate tenacity of life in terms of survival.

Take for example the Dryopithecus, first found in France in 1856, has been dated from fossils found there to about 20 million years old. Its remains have subsequently been found in Africa and Asia was well as Europe. While this animal was largely arborial and ate nuts and berries, Dryopithecus was not a knuckle walker, like the modern African apes and had a semi-erect posture.

This archaic ape is generally thought to be an ancestor of modern African apes and man. Its skeleton is similar to that of the Sivapithecus which we have already discussed as the ancestor of orangutans.

We have also talked about the Proconsul, the early ape that may have been the ancestor of the chimpanzee. Some paleontologists and anthropologists believe that Proconsul actually

Fig. 17 - *Dryopithecus and its decendant, Oreopichecus. The Oreopithecus inhabited the swamps lands of Miocene Europe and is now known to have walked on two legs.*

belongs to a subgroup of Dryopithecus.

Some scientists assert that certain aspects of bipedal movement are better explained as an adaptation to locomotion through water. Their Aquatic Ape Hypothesis (or AAH as it is called) recognizes that humans swim better than our nearest ape relatives. AAH also observes that humans exhibit some traits which are unusual among primates but are relatively common in other aquatic species and that apes actually do tend to move in shallow water in the same manner that they do on dry land (i.e. bipedally), a characteristic that is not common to other mammals.[5]

Sir Alister Hardy, a marine biologist, first proposed in the 1930s (in addition to bipedal locomotion), that several human traits, such as relatively minimal body hair and the ability to sweat moisture and salt, can be explained only through the idea that early hominids once lived in semi-aquatic environments. The hypothesis claims that our ancestors had to wade regularly through shallow water in order to procure shellfish, aquatic plants, and other potential food sources. The pertinent concept here is that with a heavy upper torso, quadrupeds would have had a more difficult time adjusting to walking upright on the savannah than in water because of natural boyancy.

The main point of the AAH hypothesis is that "many of the major physical differences between humans and the other apes are best explained as adaptations to moving (e.g. wading, swimming and/or diving) better through various aquatic media and from greater feeding on resources that might be procured from such habitats."

An extension of the AAH concept, called the AHAH theory, attempts to refine the ideas behind the Aquatic Ape view of evolutionary dynamics even farther.

Indeed, the work of some theorists, notably Marc Verhaegen, Elaine Morgan, as well as Sir Alister Hardy have suggested that the traditional paleoanthropological view of the grassland savannah origin of all bipedal primates may not be entirely accurate.

But, as usual with experts, there are differing ideas that cite a variety of causes for the development of bipedalism in man. The causal factors include: changing climate and landscape, keeping cool, sexual display and attraction, and so forth. So let us explore some of the more popular ideas in addition to the Aquatic Ape Hypothesis.

SCIENCE PHOTO LIBRARY

Procuring Food - As the African landscape gradually shifted from rainforest to large expanses of grassland savannah, archaic hominids experienced food shortages. This caused them to come down from their trees and become ground-based. Since these early humans could no longer obtain food where they lived, they were compelled to tote their food over long distances back to their home base. This would be difficult if they remained quadrupeds. Whether gatherer or scavenger, the upright posture and arms no longer needed for locomotion, enabled primative humans to carry carcasses to safe places for consumption. They also gained the ability them to see other food sources or potential danger at greater distances over the savannah grasses.

Migration - Many anthropologists believe that bipedalism developed to enable early humans to migrate to new areas. Since early hominids were compelled to leave the forest to expand into the savannah, they no longer required an anatomy suited to an arborial existance. Walking on two legs enabled them to survive because it required less energy which allowed them to travel longer distances than knuckle-walkers. As with the Procuring food hypothesis, they were also better equipped to recognize potential danger ahead and predators waiting in ambush. Other environmental factors could have contributed to an upright stance, like cold or wet ground conditions. Even today our closest primate relative, the chimpanzee will walk on two-legs temporary until it reaches dry ground while the Bili Ape, now classified as sub-species of chimpanzee, the *Pan troglodyte schweinfurthii*, does so in its swamp land habitat with considerable regularly.

The Mating Game - C. Owen Lovejoy stirred up some controversy in anthropological circles in 1981 when he suggested sex as the reason for why humans developed bipedalism. Lovejoy proposed that males that were able to walk bipedally — thus freeing their arms to carry food enticements to females — fared better in the mating game than their quadruped counterparts making them more appealing to the females. The ability to provide more food for their mates allowed them to remain home and care for their offspring, ensuring that they were able to reproduce and rear, thus evolving future generations of adept bipeds who in turn were able to pass on their genes.

Eat and Run - This hypothesis states that early humans could not have made the jump to ground-dwelling and bipedalism in one evolutionary step — which many of the previous hypotheses imply. Here the ability to walk erect was largely a serendipitous outcome of new feeding resources and methods. As our ancestors came down from the trees to forage on the ground, they adopted a squatting position to eat. Over time, physiological changes occurred in their torso, spines, and hips, causing their weight and centers of balance to shift to a lower point of the body. This offered early hominids a steadier stance as well as the ability to stand upright more easily than their quadruped relations. When our ancestors developed the need to reach higher and stand up, these physical adaptations became essential — something akin to the giraffe evolving a long neck to reach vegetation high in the trees.

Cooling Down - Walking on two feet also could have helped early hominids conserve energy. This hypotheses suggests that an erect posture protected early hominins from over-heating. According to Peter Wheeler, an evolutionary biologist, early humans were exposed to less direct sunlight on the savannah than quadrupeds of the same size. In equitorial regions, where the sun shines directly overhead, the heat load on a hominin standing erect would have been sixty percent less than that upon a quadruped. Additionally, the erect posture raised a hominins' bodies above the ground where their skin could come in better contact with cooler and faster-moving air currents. This allowed for further heat dissipation by convection, and resulted in a reduction in the need to consume water — only about three pints of water per day, whereas quadrupeds require five.

Tool Use and Making - The oldest and perhaps most popular hypothesis that attempts to explain why humans developed into bipeds states that our upright posture relates directly to our use of tools. While some researchers suggest that it was bipedalism that brought about our ability to use devices, others assert that the advent of too use caused us to become bipedal. Charles Darwin himself believed that early hominins

were "better able to defend themselves with stones or clubs, to attack their prey, or to otherwise obtain food" while standing erect, walking, and running, whereas quadrupeds of the same size are not as efficient in exerting the same force from a sitting or squatting position.

While it remains to be seen whether any of these theories emerge as a lone explaination for the whys and wherefores of human evolution and bipedal development. To my mind it is likely that there are elements of fact in all of the hypotheses mentioned here and that the causal factors of bipedalism were many.

Nevertheless, the implication of the AAH and AHAH theories in terms of Bigfoot research is that this hypothesis may offer an valid explanation for the existence of those specific hairy primate bipeds that have an affinity for water or preference for living in, or close to, aquatic environments.

Indeed, it is also interesting that the Greek hero Achilles, mentioned previously in connection with Zana, is said to have had a sea nymph as a mother. Legend states that nymphs were either of the sea or of the woodlands – which is precisely what these "heretic" theories conclude when they explore the "hybridization" of modern humans.

The application of the AAH concept to Bigfoot research also implies an explanation for Zana's proclivity for swimming and her motivation for immersing her offspring into water soon after birth.

The swamp ape and those related aquatic environs-dwelling Bigfoot animals appear to correspond to the "River Ape" concept rather well and the proclivity of the Bili Ape to walk bipedally in its swamp-land habitat lends even more credibility to the Hardy, et al, concept in this regard.

Physiological Considerations

There is considerable evidence in the form of tracks, nesting sites and other material, that cause some people to suggest that the Bigfoot is a single species of very large, hairy bipedal hominid. In fact, as we have explored in this paper, the collective term "Bigfoot" may actually represent a number of related – but distinct – primate species.

These Bigfoot, from the standpoint of a primatologist, constitute unclassified animals. They should not necessarily be thought of as an existing or extinct species of primitive ape, ape-man, or man-ape. Bigfoot could be a recently evolved member of the primate family. Thus, Bigfoot's phylogenetic origins and affiliations are open to contention within a framework of known morphology and behavior patterns for professionals that are able to maintain scientific objectivity while keeping an open mind in the face of established dogma.

Although apes, and some monkey species, are able to walk on two feet, they are routinely quadruped knuckle-walkers. No great ape (other than man) has ever been a continually upright walker as is the case in nearly all of the Bigfoot. The Bili Ape has a body similar to that of a gorilla, its facial characteristics (albeit more flat-face like a human) resemble the physiognomy of a chimpanzee. Yet, the Bili Ape seems to prefer bipedal locomotion to knuckle walking as both the chimp and gorillas do. This is perhaps an environmental adaptation to the creature's swampland habitat and seems to follow the expectations of the Aquatic Ape Hypothesis.

While the Orang Pendek may be an exception to the upright biped rule, the animal is certainly not is not a variation of the "Yeti" as the British and some international press persist to describe it. The Himalayan Yeti is physiologically different from the Indonesian Orang Pendek. My colleague, Adam Davies, has done considerable work on this variant of Bigfoot and brought back hair samples, ostensibly from the creature, which have tested out as "anomalous." But, more on the hair discoveries later in this work.

The Yeti, North American Bigfoot, the Mongolian Almas and the Chinese Kung Lu and Yeren do share the common characteristics of a shaggy coat, bipedal locomotion (at least primarily) and evasiveness, but they also have distinctive differences that prevent the pronouncement that they are the identical species. Many of the creatures appearing on my list above possess conspicuous or subtle differences that set them apart from the others.

What some "Bigfoot" creatures might actually be, zoologically, is not certain particularly in the case of those with an ursid-like body type. While Gigantopichecus is a possibility for some Bigfoot, there is no significant shred of evidence that supports this conjecture. Moreover paleontologists do not know with certainty if Gigantopithecus actually walked upright routinely or was a habitual knuckle-walker like its gorilla, orangutan and chimpanzee cousins. From some forensic reconstructions of the animal, bipedalism is unlikely. However, you must also remember that these reconstructions were developed from a few mandible, jaw and teeth fossils and not from an entire fossil skeleton.

If you were to strip the hair from the North American Bigfoot, it would likely appear more human than ape. In fact, some eyewitnesses report the Florida Swamp Ape as "a naked, hairy man" rather than an unknown creature. The pattern of dermal ridging on its hands and the human-

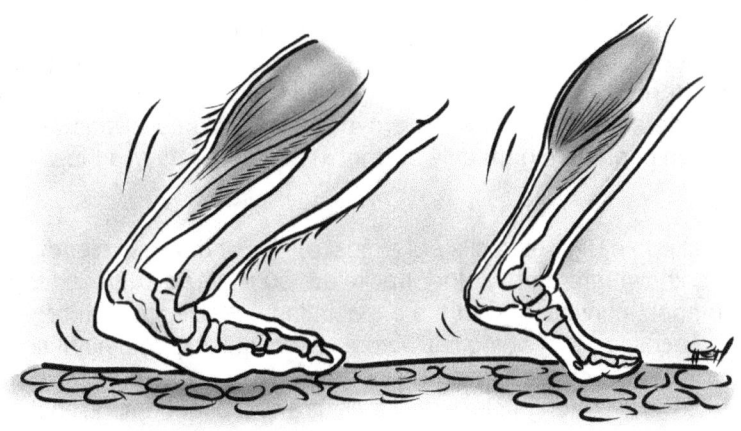

FIG. 18 - *A graphic, based on a drawing prepared by Dr. Jeffrey Meldrum of Idaho State University, illustrates the skeletal and muscular mechanics of the Bigfoot stride based on physical track evidence compared to the human stride.*

like 5-digit, parallel-toed track imprints the animal leaves behind also suggest a man-ape.

Hundreds of large humanoid footprints have been discovered around the world and dozens of them have been preserved as plaster casts or photographically. Typically, these tracks are larger than those of a human, except for those of the dwarf-type of Bigfoot. Many footprints show abnormalities common to arthritis or deformities that result from poor health and nutrition. Others possess the opposable big toe digit that is indicative of gorilla, chimpanzee, bonobo or orangutan feet.

Of the Bigfoot tracks exhibiting typical hominin traits, a sample of over 100 track casts and over 50 photographs of footprints and casts have been assembled and examined by Jeffrey Meldrum, of the Department of Biological Sciences, at Idaho State University. Meldrum also included several examples of fresh tracks in his study and analysis.

Meldrum's examination found that the Bigfoot "appear to have adapted to bipedal locomotion by employing a compliant gait on a flat flexible foot. A degree of prehensile capability has been retained in the digits by maintaining the uncoupling of the propulsive function of the hind foot from the fore foot via the midtarsal break. Digits are spared the peak forces of toe-off due to the compliant gait with its extended period of double support. This would be an efficient strategy for negotiating the steep, broken terrain … especially for a bipedal hominoid of considerable body mass, The dynamic signatures of this adaptive pattern of gait are generally evident in the footprints examined in this study."[6]

While some Bigfoot tracks are almost obvious hoaxes or clearly made by a known great ape, other tracks are considered authentic Bigfoot footprints consistent with the expectations of science with regard to the necessary physiological factors essential to bipedal hominid-type locomotion, or a feasible adaptation suited to a hominin-type creature. Moreover, it is highly unlikely that there is a conspiracy among podiatrists to concoct and plant anatomically correct, but hoaxed, tracks in extremely remote areas of the planet for unsuspecting laymen to find.

In the Northeast Malaysian State of Meghalaya a man named Nebilson Sangma came across a furry creature on a hunting trip in the jungles of the West Garo Hills in early 2002. Many people initially dismissed his account until Dipu Marak made a video record of the animal's nesting place a few days after Sangma's sighting. Zoologists and biologists shortly thereafter found unusual footprints measuring some 20 inches (50cm) in the same area.

Marak's video footage detailed signs of a Mande Burung, a Southeast Asian variety of Bigfoot.

Sangma, reported the Mande Burung had built a dwelling that it emerged from frequently to eat at a nearby banana grove. His brother, who was with Sangma during the sighting, corroborated Sagma's account. The duo viewed the events from a safe distance and reported that the sighting took place over three consecutive days.[Endnote 1]

Assuming that the Sangma account is factual, the Mande Burung ability to construct a dwelling, however crude, is the most sophisticated nesting activity among Bigfoot creatures. Most, like the Bili Ape build nests on the ground consisting of plant material like a gorilla. However the Bili Ape prefers to build its nest in swampy riverbeds.

Chimpanzees (except the Bili Ape), Orangutans, monkeys and prosimians usually nest in trees to remain safe from predators.

The North American Bigfoot and Susquatch nest on the ground like the gorillas. Their nesting sites have been found and casts have been made of the body shape of the animal from the impressions made in these nests.

The Florida Swamp Ape is said to nest inside abandoned alligator caves adjacent to rivers, streams and swamps or in layered constructs of foliage as does the gorilla and Bili Ape.

The Florida Swamp Ape is generally silent in terms of loud vocalizations, but some people claim to have heard the creature's calls late at night. The Bili Ape, on the other hand, apparently has no predators to worry about — not even human poachers will hunt them in their home environment. They are extremely strong and are called "Lion Killers" by the aboriginal tribesmen in the area. With no fear of attracting lions, leopards or hyenas, the Bili Ape hoots at the moon as it rises and sets. This behavior is extremely unusual for apes, but not for Bigfoot. The Yeti, Yowie and North American Bigfoot and others of their community also emit distinctive vocal calls. Presumably, these calls are motivated for mating purposes but could have another purpose as yet unknown.

All great apes are known for their high-pitched vocalizations when their territory is invaded or they feel threatened by humans. The exception to this rule is interestingly enough, the Bili Ape, which silently melts into the forest rather than to initiate a direct confrontation with humans.

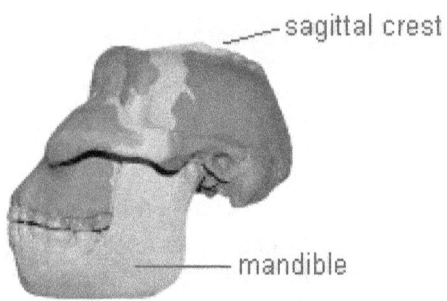

Much ado is made of a Saggital crest (see photo left) indicating that Bigfoot is related to Gigantopithecus or the Australopithecine ancestors of hominids. However this skull feature is merely an anchoring point for strong chewing muscles. In the case of the Australopithecine, this may indicate that the animal's food supply included tough plant material or that the animal was craft handy.

Native American Plains Indian women are also known to have developed this skull feature, as their lifestyle required chewing on tough buffalo hide to soften it for use in stitching together pieces of material for practical use.

The cunning and planning capacity of Bigfoot indicates that the animal is at least an omnivore, as the mental gymnastics exhibited by the creature requires a sophisticated brain. Such a brain requires significant calorie intake to function to the degree that a vegetarian diet could not support the manifest behavior of the more sophisticated Bigfoot animals.

One apparent contradiction is the Bili Ape that appears, in spite of its size, to share the chimpanzee preference for a fruit-rich diet. I believe that researchers have been too quick to pronounce the animal a vegetarian. It seems likely that further study will reveal that the Bili Ape also shares the chimpanzee predilection to hunt and devour meat. Gorillas have never been observed hunting or feeding like the chimpanzee but they are known to feed on invertebrates such as termites and ants and occasionally snails and slugs representing at least some animal protein in their diet.

There is some support for a meat-eating Bigfoot even though stories of Bigfoot attacks on bystanders are rare some accounts of this behavior do exist. There are also sightings of Bigfoot stalking or taking down animal prey like deer and killing domesticated calves.

Chimpanzee "hunts" have been documented by Jane Goodall wherein chimps stalk, trap and capture smaller primates for ingestion as food.

Recent discoveries resulting from the detailed examination of H. antecessor show that this hominid was cannibalistic due to butchering marks on its fossil remains. Other findings suggest that some of our related species also engaged in cannibalism. We already know that under extreme conditions, H. sapiens will eat its own and tribes of modern humans, until the late 20th century, practiced cannibalism in the South Pacific and elsewhere. The Agori Sect of India engages in cannibalism to this day, preferring to consume after partial cremation of a corpse.

If Bigfoot should also prove to be cannibalistic, this trait could also explain the rarity of Bigfoot fossil finds and may have a bearing on the scarcity of the creature.

Genetic Considerations of Hypertrichosis

Congenital generalized hypertrichosis (CGH) is an extremely rare genetic disorder characterized by extreme hair growth, typically on the face and upper body.

The popular press has consequently dubbed the condition the "Werewolf syndrome". Individuals with this genetic "disorder" have appeared in circuses as "dog men" and "ape men" for years (see photo right).

A table of the better known "Feral Children" appearing in historical records appears below:

Recorded Cases of Hairy Feral Children

Child Identified	Discovered in	Age at Discovery
Wolf-child of Hesse	1344	7
Wolf-child of Wetteravia	1344	12
Bear-child of Lithuania	1661	12
Sheep-child of Ireland	1672	16
Calf-child of Bamberg	d1680	?
Bear-child of Lithuania	1694	10
Bear-child of Lithuania	?	12
Kidnapped Dutch girl	1717	19
Two boys of Pyrenees	1719	?
Peter of Hanover	1724	13
Girl from Sogny	1731	10
Jean of Liège	?	21
Tomko of Hungary	1767	?
Bear-girl of Fraumark	1767	18
Victor of Aveyron	1799	11
Kaspar Hauser of Nuremberg	1828	17
Sow-girl of Salzburg	?	22
Child of Husanpur	1843	?
Child of Sultanpur	1843	?
Child of Sultanpur	1848	?

Child Identified	Discovered in	Age at Discovery
Child of Chupra	?	?
Pig-boy of Holland	?	?
Wolf-child of Holland	?	?
Wolf-child of Sekandra	1872	6
Child of Sekandra	1874	10
Wolf-child of Kronstadt	?	23
Child of Lucknow	1876	?
Child of Jalpaiguri	1892	8
Child of Batsipur	1893	14
Child of Sultanpur	1895	?
Feodor Adrianovitch Jefticheff	1895?	From Birth
Snow-hen of Justedal	?	12
Amala of Midnapore	1920	2
Kamala of Midnapore	1920	8
Leopard-child of India	1920	?
Wolf-child of Maiwana	1927	?
Wolf-child of Jhansi	1933	?
Leopard-child of Dihungi	?	8
Child of Casamance	1930s	16
Assicia of Liberia	1930s	?
Confined child of Pennsylvania	1938	6
Confined child of Ohio	1940	?

Child Identified	Discovered in	Age at Discovery
Gazelle-child of Syria	1946	?
Child of New Delhi	1954	12
Gazelle-child of Mauritania	1960	?
Ape-child of Teheran	1961	14
Genie, U .S .A.	1970	2

Although there are a number of archetypal families, such as the Jefticheffs previously mentioned, the recent "discovery" of a multigenerational Mexican family with many members manifesting this disorder has provided contemporary researchers with a rare opportunity to track the gene responsible for the condition directly.

Previous indirect studies had concluded that there is an autosomal dominant pattern of inheritance with CGH. Segregation analysis has shown that affected women can transmit the trait to both their male and female offspring.

The hair growth is typically more extreme in males. Affected females generally have a more irregular pattern of excessive hair growth. But, this is not always the case. As a result of these findings researchers now conclude that the condition is due to an X-linked dominant pattern of inheritance.

After isolating the genomic DNA the latest research genotyped CGH using PCR based hypervariable microsatellites. With these new technologies the investigators localized the causal gene to an interval between the Xq24-q27.1 region of the X-chromosome. So the latest research indicates that CGH is a fully penetrant X-linked dominant trait.

Normal hair growth is controlled by an intricate interplay of genetic and endocrine gland factors. Most forms of "hirsutism" are linked to hormone imbalances bound to locations in the body under androgen control. By contrast, hypertrichosis can include any area of the body and is caused by an acquired, or genetic, cause.

Retinoic acids and growth factors all appear to be involved in the production of hair, and we are learning more about autosomal or X-linked genes that control hair growth as research continues to study the mechanisms behind it. But the fact that other primates have substantially more hair coverage on their bodies strongly suggests that the genes responsible for hair growth have undergone some important structural or regulatory change during the evolution that resulted in modern Homo sapiens.

Thus, researchers have postulated that CGH is a manifestation of a genetic atavism- reappearance of an ancestral phenotype.

The reappearace of ancestral characteristics in individual members of our species "reminds us that the genetic and developmental information originally used in the production of such characteristics has not been lost during evolution, but lies quiescent within the genome and in the processes of embryonic development," notes Brian K. Hall, of the department of biology at the University of Halifax, Nova Scotia.

In short, this particular genetic mutation evokes a natural pattern that has been suppressed in the genetic makeup of H sapiens. Just as the loss of appendages on snakes or tails in apes, this does not mean that the ability to produce these forms has been lost. The spectacle of a three-toed horse, or a whale with hind limbs, actually represents the reappearance of anatomy previously "lost" in the process of natural selection.

So, we can postulate that the hairiness of Jo Jo and the other "wolf men" and "ape men" mentioned above is due to carrying a gene that was passed to them through heredity from ancestors that may be related to apparently kindred primates.

Assuming that Zana was indeed one of these primates, as the accounts of her suggest, her descendants carry this genetic pre-disposition for hypertrichosis. Should these offspring marry someone else that carries the gene, and bear children, the condition will re-emerge in future generations of their progeny.

It would be interesting to examine the genealogy of the Jefticheff family (and that of others manifesting hypertrichosis) to ascertain if there are any hereditary links to Zana – given that Adrian Jefticheff hails from the same general locality.

Bigfoot Hair

During my research for this book, I looked into the possible origins, speaking from an evolutionaey point of view, of this creature.

Eventually, I focused on a particular branch of the ape family tree originating with the Dryopithecus, the progenitor ape previously mentioned. This genus of ape, as I related previously, is known from the fossil record as inhabiting Eastern Africa into Eurasia during the late Miocene period. Its philogenic branch of the ape family tree was, at the time of its discovery, in a state of flux and some confusion.

Nevertheless, this creature was the ancestor of the Oreopithecus (a swamp dwelling semi-aquatic ape that ranged around the Mediterranean basin and the Ramapithecus -- an ape that was was long believed to be the first branch of apes which eventually evolved into modern man.

Tofay, the Ramapithecus is no longer thought to be a human ancestor and has been regrouped as the "Shivapithecus." It is now considered to be one of the ancestors of the orangutan and a relative of the Gigantopithecus.

As you probably know, the Gigantopithecus (is identified by many Bigfooters to be the species which gave rise to the Yeti, Sasquatch, Yeren and other Bigfoot. (Although some Russian cryptozoologists insist that these creatures are actually manifestations of the human predecessor species H, Neanderthalensis).

The Gigantopithecus ostensibly migrated into North America from Asia over the Bering Land Bridge (right) to populate North America becoming

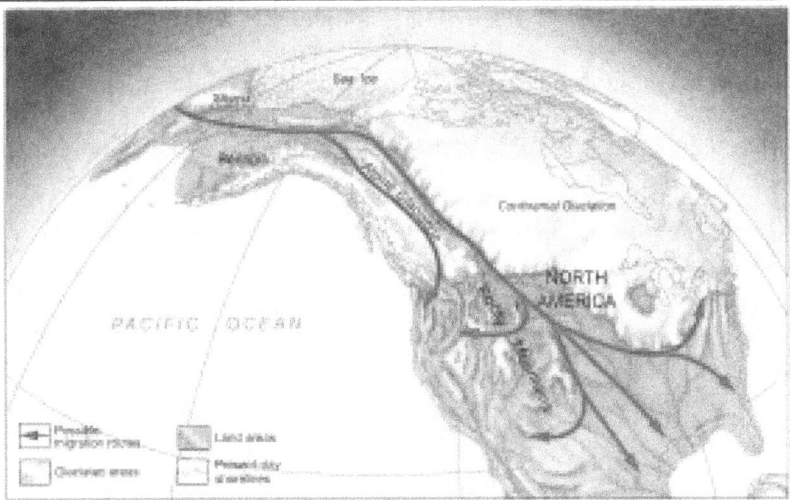

today's Bigfoot as it is known on the Pacific Coast and elsewhere in North America (see map above).

But, what scant physical evidence exists bothered me. I was (and remain) sufficiently impressed by the differences in track evidence to conclude that there are significant anatomical differences in the North American Swamp Ape, as it is known along the Gulf Coast, to distinguish it as a separate species of Bigfoot from the Sasquatch.

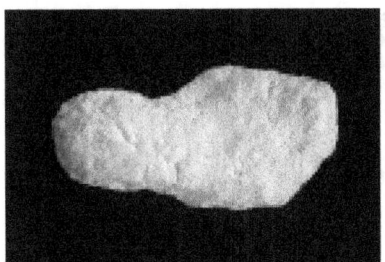 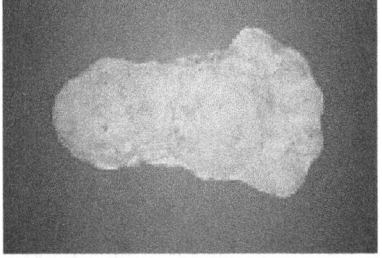

Fig. 19 - *A Swamp Ape track from Florida compared to a print casting from a Sasquatch taken in the Pacific Northwest. Note the differences in anatomy, particularly in shape and total construction.*

Consequently I put forth a hypothesis here suggesting that the origin of the Swamp Ape is actually the Oreopithecus which I maintain migrated westward through Europe and Canada and down into South America along the coastline (see mape below). Of course the evidence of this migration is no longer accessible due to sea level fluctuations since the Miocene period.

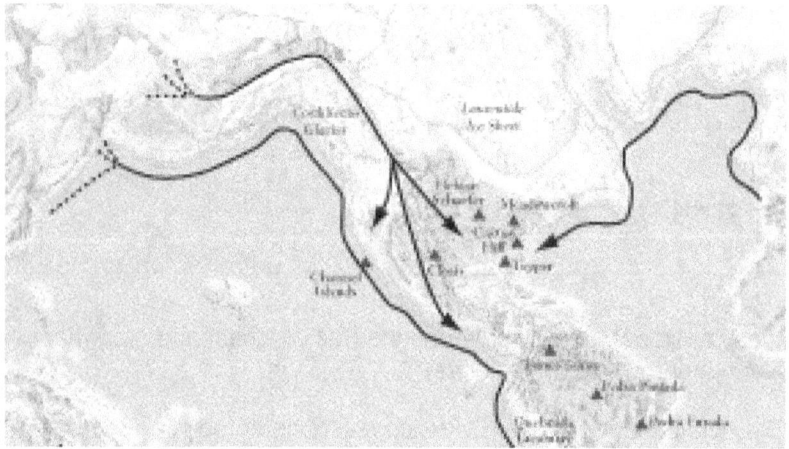

These same sea level changes facilitated the eastward migration of its cousin, the Gigantopithecus, over the Bering Sea Land Bridge.

During a cryptozoology practicum which I taught in the field, some of my students and I with cryptozoologist friend and associate, Ken Gerhard, discovered nests that resembled those made by the recently discovered Bili Ape of Africa on the ground. These nests were constructed with native flora (some of which had been brought in from a distance) and topped with a layer of Spanish moss. We took samples of the materials back to the lab at the college where I subsequently discovered hairs among the Spanish Moss.

I extracted and stored these hairs until an appropriate time to have them tested after examining them myself.

The time wasn't right then, a well-known hoaxter was involved in one of his fiascos claiming to have a Bigfoot trapped in a garage on the West Coast. The physical evidence offered was, at best, controversial. So, not wanting to reveal our hairs in the middle of that Hullabaloo, I retained the hair specimens until I could document them in a way that charges of evidence tampering would not be an issue. I had examined them myself and knew that they were significant and did not want them to be dismissed easily by skeptics as part of the protracted "hoax" going on at the time.

A proper opportunity for revelation came during the filming of a television episode on the Swamp Ape I did for the Discovery Channel. I gave the hair sample to show host, Chuck Nice, while on camera along with the chain of evidence document on them. The producers took the samples immediately to Michael Hughes at the University of Southern California.

In the photo (rigtht) I present the Swamp Ape Mystery Hair sample to host, Chuck Nice, on camera in "Is it True?" for Discovery Channel

Hair protein can be as unique as a fingerprint in identifying animals. Measurements associated with the medula, cuticle and cortex and the scale patterns appearing on the shaft of hair (see illustrationh right) in addition to its thickness are used forensically to identify species.

Dr. Hughes , a forensic hair specialist. tested the hairs for the television episode and determined they were from an unknown North American animal or from an animal from some other geographic location after comparing them to all the known species in his hair sample database.

His findings were all revealed in the episode which aired on American TV.

Jane Goodall, in one informal poll at least, is considered one of the top five most recognized living scientists. A primatologist and conservationist, Dr. Goodall has devoted almost half a century to the study of chimpanzee behavior in Tanzania and has achieved worldwide recognition for her animal advocacy.

Dr. Goodall has appeared in films and quite a number of television programs about her work, including National Geographic, HBO, PBS, and Discovery Channel's Animal Planet.

In a radio interview on National Public Radio's "Talk of the Nation" on September 27, 2002, Dr. Goodall asserted, to the surprise of the listening audience, her belief that large undiscovered primates such as the Yeti, Sasquatch, Almasty, Swamp Ape and other Bigfoot creature's actually exist.

A transcript of that portion of that radio program follows:

> **Caller:** It's a pleasure to speak with you. I wanted to know if you believe that there are any undiscovered large ape species and if you believe that the bobobo chimpanzee is a sub-species of chimp or a separate species?

<Skipping ahead to the pertinent portion of Dr. Goodall's response>

> **Dr. Goodall:** As for the other, you're talking about a Yeti or Bigfoot or Sasquatch.

> **Ira Flatow:** Is that what he's talking about?

> **Dr. Goodall:** Yes, it is and...

> **Ira Flatow:** Is that the message I'm missing here?

> **Dr. Goodall:** I think that's the message you're missing and...

> **Ira Flatow:** (To the caller) Is that right?

> **Caller:** Pretty much.

> **Ira Flatow:** (Laughing) I'm out of the loop. Go ahead.

> **Dr. Goodall:** Well now, you'll be amazed when I tell you that I'm sure that they exist.

> **Ira Flatow:** You are?

> **Dr. Goodall:** Yeah. I've talked to so many Native Americans who all describe the same sounds, two who have seen them. I've probably got about, oh, thirty books that have come from different parts of the world, from China from, from all over the place, and there was a little tiny snippet in the newspaper just last week which says that British scientists have found what they believed to be a yeti hair and that the scientists in the

Natural History Museum in London couldn't identify it as any known animal.

Ira Flatow: Wow.

Dr. Goodall: That was just a wee bit in the newspaper and, obviously, we have to hear a little bit more about that.

Ira Flatow: Well, in this age of DNA, if you find a hair there might be some cells on it.

Dr. Goodall: Well, there will be and I'm sure that's what they've examined and they don't match up. That's what my little tiny snippet says. They don't match up with DNA cells from known animals, so -- apes.

Ira Flatow: Did you always have this belief that there., that they, that they existed?

Dr. Goodall: Well, I'm a romantic, so I always wanted them to exist. (Chuckles.)

Ira Flatow: (To the caller) Alright?

Caller: Thank you.

Ira Flatow: Thanks for calling. (To Goodall) Well, how do you go looking for them? I mean, people have been looking, right? It's not like, or has this just been, since we don't really believe they can exist, we really haven't really made a serious search.

Dr. Goodall: Well, there are people looking. There are very ardent groups in Russia, and they have published a whole lot of stuff about what they've seen. Of course, the big, the big criticism of all this is, "Where is the body?" You know, why isn't there a body? I can't answer that, and maybe they don't exist, but I want them to.

Dr. Goodall reiterated her position on the existence of Bigfoot on WAMU FM radio as recently as September 9, 2009.

Now, as a scientist, Dr. Goodall well knows that anecdotal evidence is not acceptable proof for an animal's existence. Nevertheless she relies upon native folktales to base her belief (albeit a 'romantic' one) in the existence of Bigfoot.

As a colleague of the late Dion Fossey, Dr. Goodall is probably well aware that the mountain gorilla of Rwanda was an enigmatic legendary animal until 1902 when the body of one was bought back to Europe and scientifically described. While the western lowland gorilla had been known since the fifth century BC this was not the case for the mountain gorilla.

The discovery, in central Africa, of the bipedal hairy primate, known as the Bili or Bondo Ape (which I've already mentioned), that DNA analysis has confirmed is a sub-species (Pan troglodytes schweinfurthii) of chimpanzee.

The Bili Ape was known colloquially as "the lion killer" or "N'goloko" to native Africans in the vicinity of its discovery for generations before its scientific confirmation.

Dr. Goodall, in her interview on NPR, mentioned Yeti hair (see photo right) that had been discovered and was undergoing testing. Actually this is not the first time hair, ostensibly belonging to a Yeti, has been discovered. The first such sample was brought back to Britain by Sir Edmund Hillary -- the famed mount Everest explorer.

The hair sample Dr. Goodall referred to was gathered from a cedar tree in Bhutan in a forest located in the eastern part of the country. The sample was subsequently examined by Dr. Bryan Sykes, professor of human genetics at the Oxford Institute of molecular medicine, who is considered one of the world's leading experts on DNA analysis. At the time the tests done on the hair were inconclusive due to more primitive DNA technology than exists today.

More recently Yeti hair samples were brought back to Britain from northern India and tested by scientists in Redmond. The Redmond lab states that the hairs are similar to those found by Sir Edmund Hillary. Microscopic examination of the hairs have confounded the forensic team and DNA test results are pending. However experts have gone on record stating that the hairs have similarities to human hair but have significant differences as well. These experts have suggested that the hair samples are likely from a large non-human primate. And still more recent hair finds by the television team of producers of TV show "Destination Truth" for the SyFy Channel has achieved similar results.

Even before the latest round of Yeti hair discoveries two different sets of hair were collected in the Blue Mountains east of Walla Walla, Washington and attributed to the North American Sasquatch. The samples were found on freshly twisted tree limbs and associated with the sighting of a Bigfoot and tracks associated with them.

The hair samples were sent to Dr. Wolf Henner Fahrenbach in Beaverton, Oregon who examined them microscopically and determined that they came from two separate individuals of the same species based on differences in color and hair growth cycles. Fahrenbach found the samples to be indistinguishable from human hair and sent them on to Ohio State University for DNA testing.

Dr. Paul Furst at the Department of the Molecular Genetics lab at OSU performed the tests but was unable to generate a diagnostic sequence of mitochondrial genes which would have determined a relationship between a Sasquatch and other primates.

Dr. Jeff Meldrum has obtained hair samples presumed to be from the Canadian Bigfoot.

More recently Cryptozoologist, Adam Davies, has discovered hair specimens from the Orang Pendek of Southeast Asia.

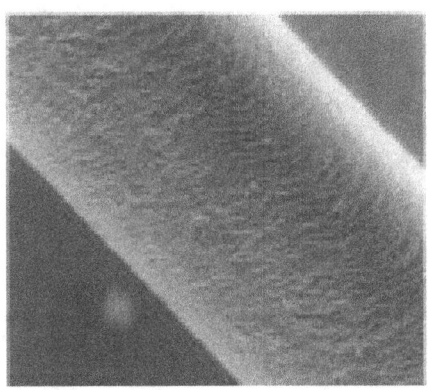

Orangutan hair (see photo left) as seen under an electron microscope, Note scale pattern

All of these hairs have been tested as anomalous.

Only recently has DNA extraction science developed the means to extract DNA from hair without the root follicle. Davies' hair has been preliminarily tested and shows a relationship to the orangutan but it is not, according to one test, from an orangutan.

This finding appears to bear out my hypothesis that (at least) some Bigfoot creatures are indeed related to the Shivapithecus. I suspect that DNA tests, when performed, on the subject hair samples from other geographic locations will yield similar results.

There is a legend told by the Paiute Native Americans about "Red-Haired Giants"who lived in North America before this tribe arrived. According to the legend, the Piautes competed with these more primitive natives for scant resources. Ultimately, the Paiutes trapped the Giants in a cave and started a fire at its entrance to suffocate their larger, but fewer, competitors.

The story could be chalked up to fanciful folklore if it were not that skeletons belonging to unusually large "people" were indeed found by anthropologists working the cave site in Nevada. The Lovelock Cave Skulls (see photo right) were recently revealed on Erich von Däniken's "Ancient Aliens"  television series but had been known to anthropologists prior to that public display.

I suspect that these anomalous skeletal remains somehow fit in to my phylogenetic hypothesis. This thought can be tested if DNA were extracted from the Humboldt skeletal remains of the so-called Red-Haired Giants to see if they are of human or of some alternate origin.

Unfortunately, communication with the museum regarding this possibility resulted in a bureaucratic run-around climaxing with the skulls being whisked away under the provisions of the Native American Repatriation Act.

Fortunately I have since discovered another cache of these bones in an ossuary controlled by a leading educational institution on the West Coast.

Permit me to elaborate on the reason that I consider these skeletal remains pertinent to the point I'm making here.

I'm troubled by the willingness to attribute all Bigfoot phenomenon to archaic humans such as the Neanderthal or Homo heidelbergensis. There are some accounts of Almasty (Central Asian Bigfoot) trading with travelers along the Silk Road. There is the story of Zana and similar accounts from parts of Asia and the Near East. These would seem to support the Human/Bigfoot attribution.

Anthropologists have discovered numerous examples of Neanderthal art and culture. Some artifacts are amazingly sophisticated. Yet, the most striking aspect of most Bigfoot encounters reported is that these creatures lack any advanced lithic technology. Indeed it is even rare to hear an anecdote about a Bigfoot event where the creature even brandishes a tree branch or club as a weapon -- much less a spear or bow and arrow.

Yet, and all but totally covered up by mainstream archaeologists, Ruth Simpson -- with the support of Lewis Leaky -- excavated an area in the Calico Mountains of California and found what appears to be lithic tools akin to those uncovered by Leaky in the Oldivai Gorge of Africa belonging to prehistoric man. These t"ools" have been dismissed by archaeologists as "site picked" and not actual litic tools. I disagree.

According to the Paiute legend the Red-Haired Giants stature was as tall as 12-feet. They were a "vicious, unapproachable people" that slaughtered and ate captured Paiutes as food" -- a habit that Paiute society found extremely unacceptable.

Yet, these paleo-indians were picked off by the Paiutes until the remnants of their "tribe" were cornered and killed a 40 by 60 foot cave cowering in fear after a few of them were ambushed while attempting escape.

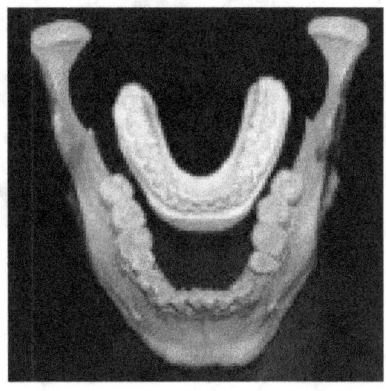

Fig. 20 - *The mandible of a Red-Haired Giant with that of a normal human.*

This is no early North American David and Goliath story. The Giants were not superior in number, despite their fearsome size and reputation. They were apparently not well-armed, when compared to the Paiutes, and were not taken down by a simple sling and a pebble.They were undone by apparently superior technology and guile.

My suspicion is that, if an ancestor of Gigantopithecus had indeed migrated to North America and evolved into a contemporary Bigfoot animal, the Red-Haired Giants make a plausible candidate for their descendents.

These giants have at least two physical traits in common with what may be their ancestral species -- unusual height and build (a characteristic perhaps inherited from the Gigantopithecus) and red hair (a normal hair coloration for an orangutan).

At Lovelock, two of the specimens recovered were mummified and thus presumably retained their orangutan red hair. I'd like the opportunity to compare this hair with that found by Adam Davies and human hair to ascertain similarities and differences.

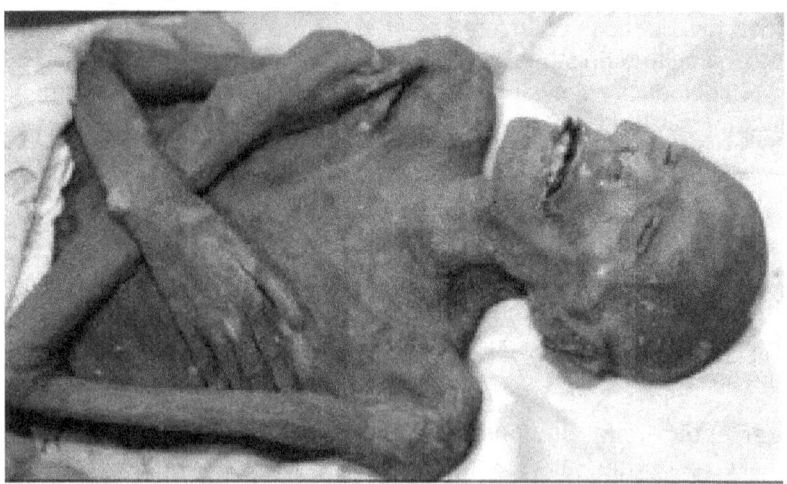

Fig. 21 - *A mummy of one of the "Red-Haired Giants" from Lovelock Cave, Nevada. This specimen rests in a museum collection, but the US government is keen to "repatriate" such remains to the Native American community rather than permit the sutdy of them.*

Which brings me to the issue of bipedalism. recent work by Spanish physical anthropologists have determined that the Oreopithecus had gained bipedal locomotion abilities, (perhaps due to their semi-aquatic habitat -- giving the nod to the Aquatic Ape Hypothesis of Elaine Morgan) 4.5 million years before our human ancestor "Lucy." Similarly the Shivapithecus was thought to have bipedal abilities.

Although neither of these apes, or their immediate descendents, likely walked on two legs habitually as did/do human species (we know that today's ape species -- including the orangutan -- are able to walk short distances on two legs). Bigfoot creatures do seem to walk erect most of the time, but there are stories in which these creatures dropped to all fours from time to time.

A species not directly related to modern humans would not necessarily evolve bipedal locomotion identical to the mechanics of the human stride due to underlying skeletal architecture differences, This thought dovetails nicely with Dr. Jeff Meldrum's analysis of Bigfoot locomotion mechanics.

Although the principal anatomy may be the nearly identical, specific nuances would result in significant differences that would be reflected in the tracks left in the ground behind. Of course, this is exactly what we see when we compare Bigfoot tracks to those of a human.

Another clearly humanoid trait has to do with dentition. In this case there is a marked reduction in the size of canine teeth in humanoid species. In fact, this was one of the traits that initially confused physical anthropologists in the classification of early pithecines with human species. Gigantopithecus and Oreopithecus both exhibit less prominent canine teeth. This too is consistent with the typical Bigfoot sighting report.

Presumably this trait would be passed on to gehetic descendents of these animals.

Some researchers have suggested that these Red-Haired Giants are the biblical Nephalim - the progeny of the "sons of God" and the "daughters of men" mentioned in to Genesis 6:4; and thus the giants who inhabited Canaan according to Numbers 13:33. I find this rush to qualify them thus as nonsense and certainly non-science. We don't have any genome, nor any hard evidence to support such a claim. Attempting to disguise this attribution with flawed DNA suggesting

BIGFOOT FAMILY TREE

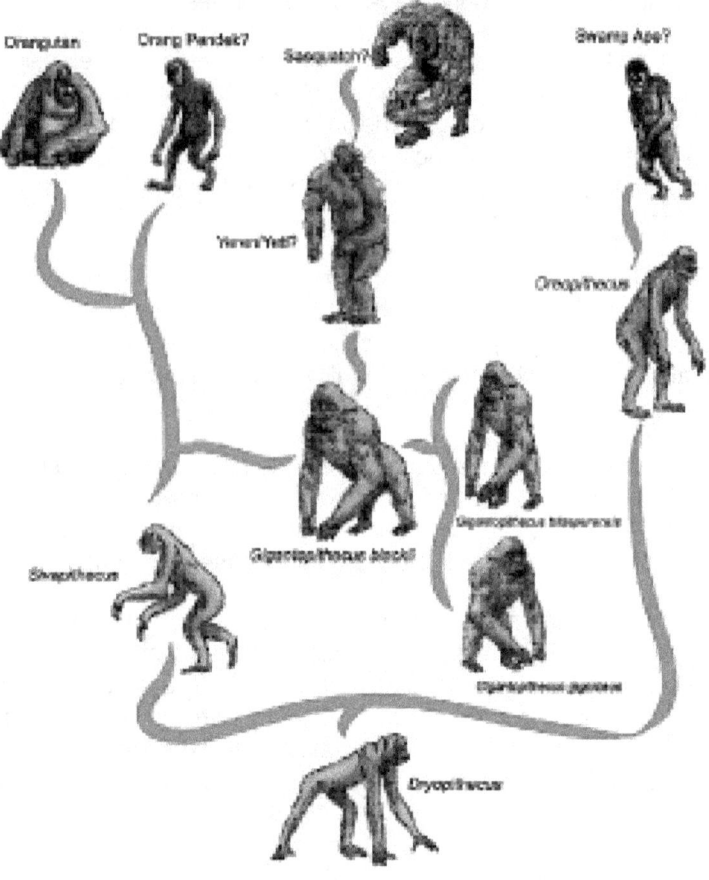

Illustration by Peter Loh

some sort of hybridization with maternal mitochondrial DNA from a modern human woman and anomalous paternal DNA is indicative of bad lab work and deliberate misinformation intended to support a religious agenda and not scientific advancement.

One of the principal objections by Bigfoot skeptics has been the notion that fossil remains of the big, hairy beast "don't exist." Thus, they reason, the animal does not exist either. Assuming that the Dryopithecene Family Tree is the paleontological basis for these creatures after all, this objection is overcome.

Another objection is that current thinking about Bigfoot and its origins consist only of speculation and assumptions which are not easily tested emphirically. My theory, as presented here, provides cryptozoology with an expanded basis against which researchers can test physical evidence obtained within a viable scientific framework of taxonomy about this enigmatic creature or creatures.

However, there is a 'but.' Much to the dismay of skeptics, this theory presumes that there are more than one species of enigmatic primate roaming the wilds of the world. Nevertheless, physical evidence collected by field researchers that appears to be credible points to this as a probability. The 'but' to the 'but' is that there is also considerable evidence that a good number of Bigfoot sightings result from cases of mistaken identity.

Take the case of the aforementioned Bili Ape, a.k.a.'N'goloko,' which was an enigmatic primate in central Africa until recently. One could argue that this animal constitutes evidence of a Bigfoot creature that had been misidentified. In this instance the mythical Ngoloko turned out to be a gargantuan member of the Pan troglodyte family. The animal's remains sat on the shelf of a museum -- incorrectly identified for 100 years -- before modern scientists corrected the misidentification error.

It would indeed be ironic if "proof" for the existence of Bigfoot had been under the nose of science all along as it was for the Bili Ape.

Thus, expanding on my concept I'm proposing a tentative phylogenetic chart for the Bigfoot family originating with the fossil species Dryopithecus -- an ancestor of the great apes -- leading through other known paleontological discoveries to different species of Bigfoot animals 'known' today.

This chart expands on ideas originating with anthropologist Grover Krantz and others which suggested a single lineage for Bigfoot.

continuing research will certainly fill in some gaps and make necessary corrections to this starting point. Cryptozoology now has the benefit of a phylogenetic framework within which to test discoveries and physical evidence.

Behavioral Traits

The reported behavior of Bigfoot has ranged from a relatively harmless response to humans to the absolutely abnormal. Typical encounters involve behaviors like tossing pebbles or wood from a distance, throwing feces, pacing a person or chasing someone. There are occasionally more aggressive contact behaviors involving shaking vehicles, and smacking or jostling buildings. Loud, resonant vocalizations are reported from time to time. In the case of the Florida Swamp Ape (AKA appropriately the "Skunk Ape") and in some Bigfoot sightings a pungent odor has also been reported.

The Bili Ape, more often than not, makes no sound and silently slips away out of sight when confronted by a human.

The Florida Swamp Ape and the American Sasquatcfh share an intimidation behavior that is apparently related to territory defense. When a human encroaches on its territory it will silently pace the perceived foe up to the point of getting so close to its antagonist that it can hear Bigfoot breathing. Yet, it will generally not allow itself to be seen.

In 1971, David Holly and a friend were on an island in Broken Bow Lake near Paris, Texas when they noticed they were being followed. At first, the duo thought the animal could be a bear so they started to run toward their boat. But soon, they could hear heavy breathing behind them. Holley turned and saw that the pursuing animal was gorilla-like with reddish-brown hair color standing erect and about 7 feet in height.[7]

The two men ran to their boat and quickly launched it into the lake. However, the creature followed them part way into the water before turning back toward land.[Endnote 2]

I have a similar account of Florida Swamp Ape conduct in my files of this particular Bigfoot's territorial defense response. However, in this nocturnal case, the animal took great pains to remain out of sight but permitted the frightened individual it was pursuing to hear its footsteps and heavy breathing. It also appeared to be photophobic of artificial light sources and remained in the shadows when the frightened individual got to an illuminated area.

To find similar examples to the Bigfoot behaviors described above in the non-Bigfoot animal kingdom, one only has to review known primate behavior: specifically, monkeys, apes, and humans.

Jane Goodall and her colleagues record many examples of chimps throwing large and small rocks at perceived threats in their book *The Chimpanzees of Gombe*.

Workers at Disney's Animal Kingdom refer to an incident where one of their male lowland gorillas threw feces at a guest who was harassing the animal as "The Bridge Incident". Chimpanzees, orangutans and some monkey species are also known to engage in this behavior in zoological parks.

In *Gorillas in the Mist*, the famed Dion Fossey reports that mountain gorillas sometimes emit a "gagging" odor. George Schaller's Mountain Gorilla relates instances where apes throw and beat on things, stamp their feet and so forth.

Both John MacKinnon (*In Search of the Red Ape*) and Birute Galdikas (*Reflections of Eden*) report that orangutans drop branches on, or push impediments towards, people invading their perceived territory.

Accounts of Bigfoot creatures possessing, using or making tools are rare. I have already stated that Zana exhibited behavior that resembles knapping – making stone flake tools from rocks. However, some accounts do state that a Bigfoot animal in thje form of the Woderose, Wildman or Wood Eater of Europe used tools.

In support of this, there is the r rendernmg of this behavior appearing (circa 1500) displayed in the National Gallery of Art in Washington, DC a woodcut by the German engraver, Hans Burgkmair I (1473–1531), entitled "The Fight in the Forest" which depicts what appears to be a Bigfoot creature brandishing a club in an altercation with a knight that is wielding a broadsword.

In terms of social development and technology, a higher primate a like New World hominin would probably have lagged behind its African,

Asian and European counterparts. This is due to the same kind of hunter/gatherer issues detailed by Dr. Jared Diamond as the cause of the developmental differences between the people of the New Guinea highlands and those that originated in the Fertile Crescent.[8]

If you pay close attention to the range of known ape behaviors you'll find them all present in the credible Bigfoot sighting accounts.

The problem is that people readily accept the reports made by recognized animal experts concerning apes in exotic locales. But, researchers are often unwilling to take reports of ape-like behavior seriously when these behaviors are reported by a layperson – particularly when a sighting has been sensationalized by irresponsible media coverage.

Russian researchers, working (again) in the Caucasus Mountain region, have documented eyewitness accounts that paint a more refined picture of Bigfoot behavior.

Local people relate numerous anecdotes of apparent familiarity between humans and these creatures. Their accounts, some of which date back hundreds of years, describe the Almas Bigfoot as able to communicate with humans by means of gestures. There are even stories of these creatures bartering food for trinkets. I have already mentioned an Italian legend where a "wildman" became a confidant of the townsfolk in a Northern Italian village during the 15th or 16th century.

These stories are quite human taken at the surface. But they are also consistent with primate behavior. Koko, a gorilla born at the San Francisco zoo, was taught to use American Sign Language (a gestural form of communication) and signs her thoughts and desires to her trainers. She has conducted an online "chat session" on AOL (through her trainer) answering questions posed by chat room guests. Koko even has her own e-mail account (koko@gorilla.org).

More to the point, Koko has demonstrated that she is able to coin words of her own using her 1,000 word ASL vocabulary as a basis to designate "water bird" as the term for "swan".

Koko's abilities are not unique, nor are they confined to members of her species that have begun life in the company of humans. Her male counterpart, Mike, was captured in the wild and has also been successfully taught to use ASL. Moreover, Mike has related information to her trainer that indicates he has retained long-term memory of his capture and the deaths of his parents at the hands of his captors.

Recent studies at a prosimian primate center located near Myakka, Florida strongly suggest that lemurs (our earliest primate relative) are able to recognize the concept of numbers, showing awareness that an object previously shown them is missing after a cover is removed to reveal the objects beneath. (The missing object is secretly taken from the items shown through a hidden trap door). The lemurs display confusion and surprise when the item turns up missing.

Thus, it doesn't seem particularly unusual that a primate as sophisticated as Bigfoot could conduct rudimentary communication or trade with human counterparts.

Conclusions

Were it not for the worldwide distribution of Bigfoot reports and the frequency of sightings by people who are unfamiliar with each other and thus, unlikely to hatch a fraud scheme, we could easily dismiss the creature as fantasy. Even with the access to mass media, one could propose that Bigfoot sightings were merely "copycat" phenomena. However, Occam's Razor (the simplest answer is usually the correct one) cannot be applied with confidence as regards Bigfoot's existence as the animal appears in colloquial myth, legend and folklore for thousands of years.

Although some photographs in support of the creature exist; none of these graphics can be considered conclusive or completely reliable evidence. Indeed, even the famed Patterson-Gimlin film of the American Bigfoot of the Pacific Northwest, is continually debated as analysis of the film continues with no conclusive determination made to either confirm its authenticity or reveal it as a hoax.

At this time, the anecdotal accounts of Zana, the Minnesota Iceman, and the Beatty wildman best demonstrate the genetic proximity of these creatures to man and their apparently close hominin affinity such that hybridization is possible between them and our own species. Indeed, the connection of a genetic trait (hypertrichosis) to Bigfoot creatures and the condition's apparent ability to manifest in hybridized Human-Bigfoot progeny seems to support this concept.

While the encounters described in the previous paragraph attribute the Bigfoot creature to our hominin relative, H. Neanderthalensis, it is unlikely that this single species could account for all the variations in physiology derived from eyewitness accounts. So it would seem entirely possible that other relic hominins could have escaped ostensible extinction and are still roaming the planet — identified by colloquial names. As previously stated, the fossil record confirms that this was the norm thousands of years ago.

It seems fitting that the Bili Ape should turn out to be another member of the genus Pan as the Bonobo, or so-called Pygmy Chimpanzee then represents the same range of size variation found in humans – as chimps are our nearest genetic primate relation. Humans are known to exhibit size variation as an environmental adaptation and this same trait has now been confirmed in H. erectus with the Meganthropus and Floresensis at opposite extremes for this species of hominin.

So the schedule of Bigfoot animals I began this paper with also follows the variation in height/size that is apparently a commonality among hominin closely related to modern humans.

Dr. Krantz maintained that Bigfoot was most likely Gigantopithicus blacki - an obscure, giant ape-like creature whose fossil remains were found in the Yunnnan Region of China in the early 1960s.

But the fossils of this large ape, so far uncovered, consist of only a few jaw fragments and teeth. The anthropological reconstruction of a largely bipedal, 7 to 12-foot tall pongid-like creature from these scant remains is a stretch. To suggest that Bigfoot and Gigantopithicus are one-and-the-same is highly premature and likely a response to the highly-charged political climate of Krantz's day rather than good science. (Krantz paid the price in loss of tenure and ridicule for his "heresy" at avowing Bigfoot exists — much less ascribing it to the fossil record and suggesting it was an ape-man).

It is more likely that the Bigfoot of the Pacific Northwest, and other hairy bipeds known world-wide under various colloquial names, are relatives of Meganthropus — the giant sub-specie of Homo erectus (reconstructed from more complete fossil evidence — also performed by Krantz).

The African evolved and widely traveled Homo erectus is also apparently the immediate relative of the newly discovered floresiensis, the diminutive hominin recently found on the island of Flores in Indonesia. But more importantly, Floresiensis is now known to have survived at least until the last ice age on Flores about 11,000 years ago.

The evidently more adaptable Homo erectus or ergaster relatives could have survived, and possibly remain among us, in the form of the enigmatic Bigfoot and at least some of his cousins. Indeed, it seems likely to me that the Red-Haired Giants are more likely related to, if not actually H. erectus megnthropus and this potentiality should be easily confirmed by comparison of fossil remains with the skeletal remains of the giants.

In this regard, it would be helpful if researchers developed clear and distinct profiles of the various Bigfoot animals in a centralized database so that those creatures possessing significant similarities and differences could be readily identified. This would also facilitate a claudistic comparison of these animals and the subsequent placement of these creatures on a primate phylogenic chart showing probable evolutionary ancestry.

The discovery of the African Bili Ape and H. florensienses appear to demonstrate that western science has not yet discovered all the great apes that exist, or have existed, on planet Earth, as many scientists would prefer to believe. Certainly, the Bili Ape had sporadic contact with humans over the past 100 years (at least) and remained elusive until recent technologies, and a re-examination of old evidence, revealed its existence. Moreover, the radio carbon dating of H. florensienses substantiates that this hominid did survive at least until the last ice age and didn't die out concurrently with its apparent direct ancestor H. erectus.

It would certainly be helpful, in the cause of Bigfoot, to find remains containing soft tissue that would facilitate DNA analysis, and with some luck this may occur soon – given the animal's loss of habitat. Such a discovery would likely resolve the argument that the animal fails to appear in the fossil evidence. Surely some fossil remains are present, if the animal exists, or existed at one time, even if this evidence is scant, incomplete or currently misinterpreted.

Rumors persist, in zoology and cryptozoology circles, that some soft tissue remains of H. florensiensis have indeed been found. Obviously, if this is true, the creature must exist as a contemporary animal since soft tissue would not ordinarily remain intact in the tropical climate where H. florensiensis was found over the millennia.

The recent discovery of H. florensiensis does demonstrate that the size range of various legendary Bigfoot creatures around the world, from dwarf to giant, does indeed match the known variations in the family of hominins. Moreover, the existence of H. florensiensis in the geography where it was found also analogous to the traditional myth, legend and folklore surrounding the Ebo Gogo and Orant Pendek of the region is a conspicuous coincidence.

Unfortunately, there are those in the Bigfoot community that mock the "gullability" of Bigfoot "Believers" and will do just about anything to profiteer on the people and their convictions. These types do nothing to improve the public percption of those of us who seek facts concerning the creature (real or not) and an injustice to those who purchase their publications, videos, and other materials in an attempt to "entertain" us with their frauds. These few are exploiters, plain and simple, and need to be isolated and ignored by those doing genuine research. Anything else only ligitimizes the hoaxers and their cause.

Fortunately, and even in the face of this mockery, it is difficult to summarily dismiss the physiological evidence in support of Bigfoot -- given the quantity and quality of materials that have been amassed around the world that is difficult to explain away. Hair samples have been found "inconclusive" but many of the animal's tracks have been shown to fit physiological expectations – despite some obvious and more sophisticated attempts at fakery. The animal's footprints, body prints, and remains have been found to be consistent with the eyewitness descriptions of a bipedal primate.

We now have a genetic explanation for the hairiness of the creature. With the realization that all former artistic forensic renditions of human ancestors from their fossil remains can not, with 100% accuracy, predict either skin color or hair coverage on the body, it seems that we may have seen the face of Bigfoot in these representations after all – albeit clean shaven.

Perhaps the most compelling evidence in support of Bigfoot is that the behaviors reported by credible eyewitnesses are a dead-on match to the known and documented behavioral traits of Bigfoot's presumptive animal family if not its genus.

Finally, I've put forth here a possible philogeny that expands on Grover Krantz' assertion as to the status of Gigantopithecus as a progenitor of Bigfoot. This hypothesis, offers a second member of the Bigfoot family as a separate and distinct species from the "Classic" Bigfoot creature that explains why some features described by eyewitnesses differ with habitat.

Given these circumstances, it would be appropriate to continue to conduct the field studies essential to, and consistent with, establishing the conclusive existence of these creatures under the standards accepted by Western Science.

So, we come back to my original question: What is Bigfoot?

The information that we have explored in these pages is not sufficient to arrive at any absolute conclusion as to the real identity of this creature. We have, however, explored all the pottibilities that I first described and seen that they are each a plausible explanation for the Bigfoot enigma.

I think we can also conclude that holding only to the "romantic" notion that Bigfoot must be an undiscovered species is not the best science as it does not represent the kind of open mind that true science requires. This is not to say that Cryptozoology, in its current state, is not a science in and of itself. Certainly, mainstream science also tends to hold its dogma sacred and is lothe to remove its blinders to examine some phenomena with equal curiousity and a receptive consideration of new and different ideas.

Footnotes

1 Some reports suggest that the exhumation of Zana has already been accomplished by the former Russian Republic. The USSR's interest in cryptozoological studies has been well documented but the public accounts provided by the authorities deny that Zana's body has ever been found.

2 "Biologists Observe Gorillas Using Tools", Joseph B. Verrengia, AP Science Writer, September 30, 2005, http://www.plosbiology.org, Newsday, Inc.

3 "Elusive African Apes: Giant Chimps or New Species?", John Roach, National Geographic News, April 14, 2003

4 "Hobbit-Like Human Ancestor Found in Asia", Hillary Mayell, National Geographic News, October 27, 2004

5 River Apes – A Different Story About Human Evolution, *Algis Kuliukas, January 2006, http://www.riverapes.com*

6 "Evaluation of Alleged Sasquatch Footprints and Their Inferred Functional Morphology", D. Jeffrey Meldrum, Department of Biological Sciences, Idaho State University, Undated (1996?), http://www.isu.edu/~meldd/fxnlmorph.html

7 "Investigators track local reports of Bigfoot", Jeff Parish, The Paris News, March 10, 2002

8 "Guns, Germs, and Steel: the Fates of Human Societies", Jared Diamond, July 11, 2005, W. W. Norton & Company

Endnotes

1 'We Saw Bigfoot', Rahul Karmakar, The Straits Times March 25, 2002

2 "Investigators track local reports of Bigfoot", Jeff Parish, The Paris News, March 10, 2002.

Illustration Credits

All photography/illustrations included in this work is derived from public domain resources, placed there by their by their apparent copyright holders. The specific source for each photo is listed below:

Page	Position	Citation/Source
7	Center	By Peter Loh/Author
9	Center	By Peter Loh/Author
11	Top	By Peter Loh/Author
14	Top	By Peter Loh/Author
18	Top	By Author
20	Top	By Author
21	Bottom	By Author
22	Top	By Author
23	Top	Claim Photo courtesy of State Farm
24	Bottom	Deformed Bones/www.jakes-bones.com
26	Left	Roe/www.bermuda-triangle.org
28	Right	Lakeland Swamp Ape by Matt Ellis
29	Bottom	Stock Photo
30	Top	De Loy's Ape/www.bigfootencounters.com
31	Right	Altavistic Tail/evolutionfun.com
32	Top	www.europe-atlas.com
33	Bottom	Zana/www.floridaskunkape.com
34	Top	Knapping/www.ucl.ac.uk
35	Left	Khwit/http://www.phantomsandmonsters.com
35	Left	Khwit Skull/www.bigfootencounters.com

Page	Position	Citation/Source
37	Right	Khwit Skull/www.bigfootencounters.com
38	Top	Wildman Poster/www.sideshowworld.com
40	Top	Movie Poster/en.wikipedia.org
40	Bottom	Movie Photo/www.themakeupgallery.info
41	Top	Wildman/www.mtb-forum.it
41	Bottom	Wildman/freeforumzone.leonardo.it
42	Top	Family Selvatica/Smithsonian NGA
42	Bottom	Fight in the Forest/Smithsonian NGA East Wing
43	Top	Jo Jo The Wolf Boy/thehumanmarvels.com
44	Top	Mono Grande/www.bigfootencounters.com
45	Left	Stock Photo
45	Left	Stock Photo
46	Top	Bongo Ape/karlshuker.blogspot.com
47	Top	Gilgamesh Tablet 1/www.noahsarkrugs.com -
48	Top	Cylendar Seal/www.theosociety.org
50	Top	Ardipithecus/blogs.discovermagazine.com
56	Bottom	Ice Man/www.bringmethenews.com
57	Right	Nguoi Rung drawing/www.bigfootencounters.com
59	Cenrter	Russian Almasty/slobodni.net
61	Top	Yeti Hands/www.freerepublic.com
63	Top	Smilodectes Skeleton/bio.sunyorange.edu
64	Center	Foramin Magnum/anthro.palomar.edu
66	Top	Dryopithecus/frontiersofzoology.blogspot.com

67	Top	Primate Timeline/www.age-of-the-sage.org
69	Bottom	Earl;y Primates/www.jornalganapati.com.br
71	Top	Prehistoric Gatherer/frontiersofzoology.blogspot.com
73	Top	Prehistoric Tool Makerlithiccastinglab.com
75	Bottom	By Peter Loh/Author
78	Top	Saggital Crest/www.daviddarling.info
79	Bottom	Dog Faced Man Poster/www.zazzle.com.au
82	Bottom	Hirsuite Man by Peter Gonsalvu/Ambras Castle
85	Top	Beringa Migration/drarchaeology.com
85	Bottom	(Left) Swamp Ape Track from Ocala NF/By Author
85	Bottom	(Right) Bigfoot Track Northern California/By Author
86	Top	Atlantic Migration/www.davidpratt.info
87	Center	Frame Capture from Discovery Channel "Is it Real"
90	Center	Yeti Hair/news.bbc.co.uk
91	Bottom	Orangutan Hair/www.pgbeautygroomingscience.com
92	Center	Red-Haired Giant Skull/www.davidicke.com
93	Bottom	Giant Mandible/www.ancientlosttreasures.com
94	Bottom	Red-Haired Giant/yesteryearsnews.wordpress.com
96	Top	By Peter Loh/Author
105	Bottom	By Peter Loh/Author

Biographical Names Index

P

Petrova, Nadia 42
Phillips, Mike 15
Porshnev, Boris 32

R

Ripley, Robert 39
Roe, William 25

S

Sabekia, Gamasa 35
Sabekia, Khwit 35
Sanderson, Ivan T. 58
Sangma, Nebilson 76
Schaller, George 99
Schouteden, Henri 56
Scopes, John 39
Simpson, Ruth 93
Sykes, Bryan 90

T

Thompson, David 19

V

Verhaegen, Marc 70
von, Erich Däniken 92

W

Ward, Jennifer 27

Z

Zana 32

About the Author

Proclaimed, "America's most credible cryptozoologist," Scott Marlowe, is one of the few professionals in cryptozoology who works in the field as well as the laboratory and classroom.

A Fellow 0f the Pangea Institute, Marlowe also serves as the educational consultant to the American Primate Conservation Alliance, and past state delgate and former board member of the Florida Motion Picture and Television Association (Daytona Chapter).

Marlowe is one of the most sought after experts in his area of expertise. His cryptozoology course was hailed as one of the "Top Ten" news stories of 2004 by The Cryptozoologist, a well-known insider eMagazine and has received accolades and awards for his research approach and application of forensic science methodologies to the study of enigmatic animals.

Marlowe's television credits include: MonsterQuest, Is it True, Legend Hunters, William Shatner's Weird of What, Destination Truth. Weird Travels and Weird Florida in addition to countless radio appearances, TV guest spots, lecture tours and museum presentations.